STEPS
TO
HOPE

To Margaret

STEPS TO HOPE

JOYCE M. SHUTT

HERALD PRESS
Scottdale, Pennsylvania
Waterloo, Ontario

Library of Congress Cataloging-in-Publication Data
Shutt, Joyce M., 1936-
    Steps to hope / Joyce M. Shutt.
        p.   cm.
    Includes bibliographical references.
    ISBN 0-8361-3524-5 (alk. paper)
    1. Beatitudes—Devotional literature. 2. Hope—Religious
aspects—Christianity. 3. Twelve-step programs—Religious
aspects—Christianity. 4. Shutt, Joyce, 1936-   . I. Title.
BT382.S48 1990
248.8'6—dc20   90-37806
                                                                      CIP

Unless otherwise indicated Scripture quotations are from the *Good
News Bible*. Old Testament copyright © American Bible Society 1976;
New Testament copyright © American Bible Society 1966, 1971, 1976.
Scripture quotations marked (AMP) are from *The Amplified Bible*. Old
Testament copyright © 1965, 1987 by The Zondervan Corporation. *The
Amplified New Testament* copyright © 1958, 1987 by The Lockman Foun-
dation. Used by permission.
Scripture quotations marked (NEB) are from *The New English Bible*. ©
The Delegates of the Oxford University Press and the Syndics of the
Cambridge University Press 1961, 1970. Reprinted with permission.

Grateful acknowledgment is made to the following for permission to
quote from copyrighted works:
One Day at a Time in Al-Anon copyright © 1973, by Al-Anon Family
Group Headquarters, Inc. Reprinted by permission of Al-Anon Family
Group Headquarters, Inc.
Two-Way Prayer, by Priscilla Brandt, © 1979 by Word Inc., Dallas, Texas.
The Twelve Steps with the biblical comparisons are used with the per-
mission of the AA General Service Office.

To my four wonderful children.
You taught me in unforgettable ways
that we can either be "bitter"
about our trials in life,
or "better" because of them.
Together we learned that the difference
between bitterness and betterment
is one letter and one person.
"I."

Contents

Author's Preface

Several years ago, my husband and I attended our first Families Anonymous Meeting (FA). FA is a Twelve Step Program. It helps parents and family of alcoholics, addicts, and emotionally disturbed children live happy lives despite their child's addiction or illness.

Like all Twelve Step Programs, FA is essentially a spiritual program. Working with the Twelve Steps has changed our lives and stirred spiritual rebirth. Our faith has grown. Our hearts and minds have opened to the life-changing power of God. Through FA, God has given us the gift of seeing ourselves, our children, the church, and the Bible through new eyes.

Watching people go through FA has taught me a lot. I've learned it doesn't pay to be proud. I've learned we're our own worst enemies.

And I've learned humility is truly the better way.

Life often slams us on our knees. Unless we have the strength and grace bred by humility, we put ourselves or others down instead of opening ourselves to life's lessons.

Those who leave a Twelve Step program not helped can't admit their way isn't working. Those who find help can admit they need help. The program, incidentally, defines insanity as being unable to learn from experience and repeating unproductive behaviors.

I've learned it doesn't help to blame others, no matter what they've done since I can't change others. The only person I can change is myself. I can be more honest when I stop pretending life is different than it is. Then new things can happen in my life. I can let go of yesterday, stop worrying about tomorrow, and live one day at a time.

I've learned to see each sober day as a God-given reprieve from the hell we knew while our children were drinking. I've learned to believe in miracles—which happen daily as those of us in the program find healing and hope.

As a minister of the gospel I long to see more of this redemptive power unleashed in our churches. The people in our congregations are no different from those in Twelve Step Programs. Like them, our church folks are good, decent individuals. And like Twelve-Steppers, they have problems, some very serious.

In spite of our expectations, being Christian doesn't protect us from the flaws and temptations that go with living. Believers are unfaithful to spouses. They beat wives and children. They fall into depression. They suffer eating disorders. They get fired from their jobs. They become addicted, resentful, jealous, and greedy.

The tragedy isn't that Christians have problems. The tragedy is our reluctance to get help because we're ashamed to let others know what's happening to us.

Before addicted people can get help they must accept that there is no cure for their addiction. Once an alcoholic, always an alcoholic. Once a gambler, always a gambler. Once a co-dependent, always a co-dependent.

Yet all is not hopeless. Even though addictions can't be cured, they can be controlled. The first step is abstinence. The second is self-acceptance. The third is learning a better way to live.

It's the same with sin. Sin is an addiction, thus once a sinner always a sinner. Jesus came to help us say "no" to sin's seductive promises. He came to help us turn our wills and lives over to the care and guidance of our heavenly Father. Under God's care we can live happy, productive lives even though we retain the tendency to sin.

When I began using the insights the Twelve Step Program was giving me, our chaotic pain-filled home situation started to change. I discovered that problems, failure, and having alcoholic children didn't make me a bad person.

As I began accepting things as they were, I stopped judging and trying to change my children. I focused instead on ways *I* was responding to the situation and ways *I* could change. This helped change us all.

Today life for us is different. We've come a long way from the time when we were all functioning so poorly. Recovery is a process. We have a long way to go. We continue to attend our meetings and read and reread the materials which keep us on track.

Seeing how well our children are doing and how much better I feel, I'm awed at the human capacity to change. The goodness of a God who forgives and permits us to start over again and again overwhelms me.

Rarely a day goes by that I don't thank God for the gift of addiction. This is a paradox, I know. But if our lives hadn't become so chaotic and painful we never would have realized how arrogant and self-centered we all were. Every day I use something I've learned in the Twelve Step Program, not just with my family but with friends and parishioners.

Once I was ashamed that three of our four children are alcoholics. No longer. Now I see in our struggles the guiding, redeeming hand of God.

Once all I saw in our pain was my failure as a Christian and a parent. Now I'm so aware of the gift involved in the challenges life has given us, it's hard to remember that once I blamed and cursed God for making us suffer. We have grown so much in our efforts to come to terms with the roots of this terrible disease. Indeed everything does work for good for those who love the Lord!

Despite my gratitude, I still grieve. I grieve that

my children will have to fight this terrible disease for the rest of their lives. They will always be vulnerable to the allure of a quick fix or just one drink.

But when I'm tempted to yield to self-pity, I focus on the insights the disease has given us. I remind myself we could be suffering something far worse than family addictions. Most of all I'm grateful we found the program and that it has worked for us.

We take so much in life for granted! I rarely praised my family for doing anything well. I demanded of them the excellence I demanded of myself. I never questioned having a nice home, financial security, food to eat, friends, a supportive church, loving parents. Those were things one was supposed to have. How arrogant I was!

One of the things I've come to value in "the program" is that no one defines God for anyone else. That kind of openness frightened me at first. It ran counter to much of what I'd learned. I believed there was only one way to understand God. It was my job as a pastor to teach people those right beliefs and correct interpretations.

I'm learning, however, that God is so great and wonderful we can never limit God to our understandings or definitions. Each of us responds to God in our own way. In the same way, God values everyone's story and experience. What is, is.

We start where we are, then we move on. By sharing what we're learning and discovering, we encourage others to live out what makes sense to them and let the rest go. It's in that spirit that I invite you to read what I have to say.

In March 1988, God provided me with a vehicle for putting some of my new insights and enthusiasm for life into writing. With fear and trembling I delivered a series of sermons to the Grace Mennonite Church in Pandora, Ohio. These sermons form the basic outline for this book.

I had always felt safe in my home congregation at Fairfield Mennonite in Fairfield, Pennsylvania. Ours is an accepting little group. But to go into a larger church of virtual strangers and share my experience with family addictions and my rebirth through the Twelve Steps—that felt risky!

As the days of sharing unfolded I could hear Jesus say to me, "Oh ye of little faith!" I had found new insight and power in the Twelve Steps and their echoes of the Sermon on the Mount's wisdom, particularly as summarized in the Beatitudes. So too did those dear people at Grace Mennonite. Once again I learned the lesson God keeps teaching me: we communicate best when we simply tell the story of how God is working in our lives.

What follows in this book is an exploration of the Beatitudes seen through my experience and understanding of Twelve Step insights. In spite of my enthusiasm for the Twelve Steps, my faith and understanding of God remains rooted in the Bible and Jesus' teachings.

I know many in the church face the same agonies we faced when our children were actively using alcohol. My goal is to build, on my and their behalf, a bridge between the church I love and the program that has given me life.

I want others to see how the Twelve Steps and Jesus' teachings in the Beatitudes parallel each other. I want to show that the Twelve Step Program is far more than just another self-help project. It's profoundly spiritual, inspired, and shaped by God to help us build God's church in this day and age.

If your family is struggling with addictions, I want you to realize that attending Twelve Step Meetings won't violate your commitment to Christ and the church. Our experience, in fact, is that it will enhance your faith!

Addictions can afflict the most upright people and families. Some addictions are physical in origin, others psychological or spiritual, but the effects are the same. If you or someone in your church or family is suffering from compulsive behaviors, I hope this book will free you to go to FA, Alcoholics Anonymous, or some other Twelve Step Group.

My prayer is that a window or door may open for you as you read. God bless you as you look through the window or walk through the door.

—*Joyce M. Shutt*
Orrtanna, Pennsylvania

Introduction to Twelve Step Programs

Since 1936, millions of people all over the world have broken free of the addictive behaviors that enslaves them. They've done so through a spiritual program called the Twelve Steps. These steps have enabled hopeless drunks, confirmed gamblers, drug addicts, bulimics, and sufferers of various compulsive–obsessive disorders to become serene, responsible, happy persons.

For the addict and her or his family, the Twelve Step Programs are indeed a gift from God! The Twelve Step Programs are not an instant or easy cure. But they have been more successful in arresting addictions than any other treatment or approach to date.

The program enlists twelve principles which are practical, understandable, and universally applicable regardless of educational level, background, religion, or nationality. All one needs to enter the program is a desire to improve the quality of one's life. A basic grasp of language and minimal literacy skills are helpful but not essential.

Alcoholic Anonymous, better known as AA, was the first of the Twelve Step Programs. It was founded by two alcoholics, Bill Wilson and Bob Smith, in 1936. To achieve sobriety they drew on the spiritual resources they knew to be the only answer to their compulsive drinking. Wilson and Smith borrowed heavily from the work of William James, Carl Jung, William Silkworth, and Sam Shoemaker.

But the conceptual pattern and format for AA and the Twelve Steps comes from The Oxford Groups, a Christian renewal movement that was popular in the 1920s and 30s. Frank Buchman, an American Lutheran pastor, started the Oxford Groups (not to be confused with John Henry Newman's Oxford Movement) in England.

Buchman had a vision of a sin-free, Christ-led world. After converting two Cambridge University students, he challenged them to help him evangelize Oxford University. While it seemed an impossible goal, they were phenomenally successful.

Since Oxford was a crossroad for all sorts of lay and professional people, dynamic spiritual breezes quickly blew to other areas of the world. These ecumenical and nondenominational groups helped individuals find a meaningful personal relationship with Christ in the context of a caring, supportive group. They also encouraged people to appreciate their own religious traditions.

Unfortunately, the Oxford Groups died out during the World War II years. Echoes still survive, however, in the work of The Fellowship of Reconciliation and Twelve Step Programs.

Ebby T. (using only initials rather than full last names is an AA practice), an old drinking partner of Bill Wilson, found sobriety for himself after participating in one of these Oxford Groups in 1934. Wanting to share what he'd found, he witnessed to Bill W., whose advanced alcoholism had placed him on the brink of death. By now an agnostic, Bill W. was unable to open himself to the idea that God could heal him of his malady and compulsion.

In December of that same year, Bill W. was again hospitalized for acute alcoholism. In desperation, he pleaded with Ebby T.'s God to help him. God answered. Bill W. had a Pauline-type experience. Not only did he never drink again, he felt God calling him to use his own experience to help other alcoholics find sobriety.

After his conversion, Bill W. and Ebby T. faithfully attended the Oxford Groups in their area. They carried its message to fellow drunks with little success. In May of 1935, Bill W. went to Akron, Ohio, on a business trip. Tempted to drink when his business venture failed, he called a local minister and asked for names of other alcoholics he might talk to. Thus he was led to Dr. Bob Smith.

Fortunately for us all, instead of overwhelming Dr. Bob with his religious enthusiasm, Bill W. quietly shared the story of how his drinking had devastated his marriage, business, and life and how he found sobriety.

By simply telling his story, Bill W. helped Dr. Bob admit that he was powerless over alcohol, which had made his life unmanageable.

The success of this meeting with Dr. Bob prompted the specific style of AA witnessing that continues to be so powerful. "Hello. My name is. . . . I am an alcoholic."

In 1937, Bill W., Dr. Bob, and the other recovering alcoholics who were meeting with them broke with the Oxford Group. Their aim was to embrace a specific ministry to drunks.

Unlike the Oxford Group, which was specifically Christian, AA didn't ground the healing power of God exclusively in the person of Jesus. Knowing how alcoholics think and feel, they chose the words "Higher Power" instead of God. They challenged each person to reach out to a God they could accept and believe in rather than one defined for them by somebody else.

AA also backed away from pressure tactics or practices which might raise the defenses of already defensive drinkers. They quickly learned the importance of anonymity as a way of helping engender trust within the group as well as countering the moral stigma attached to alcoholism.

Even today the Twelve Step approach testifies to the dynamic witness of the Oxford Movement. Among ideas borrowed is the informality of the meetings where prayer, study testimonials, socials, and racial equality and fellowship are integral.

It's ironic that one of the most spiritually potent movements in history is still so misunderstood and even feared by religious bodies and leaders today. This spiritual movement has transformed some of the most impotent and devastated people in the world, the very people the church looks down on as lost and morally weak.

But isn't that consistent with God's way of working throughout history? Hasn't God always revealed God's presence to the poor, the disenfranchised, the outcasts? Hasn't God always dwelt among women, shepherds, slaves, foreigners, drunks, or addicts?

We in the church have much to learn from AA and other Twelve Step Groups. The movement can teach us about the nature of a caring community. It can tell us how to minister to the broken and lost without judging or condemning. Most important, perhaps, The Twelve Steps are so comprehensive in their simplicity that they can provide a stepping-stone for anyone who seeks to grow "both in body and in wisdom, gaining favor with God and men" (Luke 2:52).

Our Journey Through the Twelve Steps of Families Anonymous and Their Biblical Comparisons

(1) We admitted we were powerless over drugs and alcohol and other people's lives, that our lives had become unmanageable. "I know that good does not live in me—that is, in my human nature. I don't do the good I want to do; instead, I do the evil that I do not want to do." (Rom. 7:18-19)

(2) We came to believe a power greater than our-

selves could restore us to sanity. "If the spirit of God, who raised Jesus from death, lives in you, then he who raised Christ from death will also give life to your mortal bodies by the presence of his Spirit in you." (Rom. 8:11)

(3) We decided to turn our will and lives over to the care of God as we understood God. "Offer yourselves as a living sacrifice to God, dedicated to his service and pleasing to him." (Rom. 12:1b)

(4) We made a searching and fearless moral inventory of ourselves. "Let us examine our ways and turn back to the Lord." (Lam. 3:40)

(5) We admitted to God, to ourselves, and to another human being the exact nature of our wrongs. "So then, confess your sins to one another and pray for one another, so that you will be healed." (James 5:16a)

(6) We were ready to have God remove all these defects of character. "Humble yourselves before the Lord, and he will lift you up." (James 4:10)

(7) We humbly asked God to remove shortcomings. "But if we confess our sins to God, he will keep his promise and do what is right: he will forgive us our sins and purify us from all our wrongdoing. (1 John 1:9)

(8) We made a list of all persons we had harmed. We became willing to make amends to them all. "Do for others what you want them to do for you: this is the meaning of the Law of Moses and of the teachings of the prophets." (Matt. 7:12)

(9) We made direct amends to such people whenever possible, except when doing so would in-

jure them or others. "So if you are about to offer your gift to God at the altar and there you remember that your brother has something against you, leave your gift . . . go at once and make peace with your brother . . . ." (Matt. 5:23-24)

(10) We continued to take personal inventory. When we were wrong we promptly admitted it. "And because of God's gracious gift to me, I say to every one of you: Do not think of yourself more highly than you should. Instead, be modest in your thinking . . ." (Rom. 12:3)

(11) We sought through prayer and meditation to improve our conscious contact with God as we understood God. We prayed only for knowledge of God's will for us and the power to carry that out. "But if any of you lacks wisdom, he should pray to God, who will give it to him . . ." (James 1:5)

(12) Having had a spiritual awakening as a result of these steps, we tried to carry this message to others and to practice these principles in all our affairs. "My brothers, if someone is caught in any kind of wrongdoing, those of you who are spiritual should set him right; but you must do it in a gentle way. And keep an eye on yourselves, so that you will not be tempted, too." (Gal. 6:1)

The Beatitudes

"Happy are those who know they are spiritually
poor;
the Kingdom of heaven belongs to them!
"Happy are those who mourn;
God will comfort them!

"Happy are those who are humble;
    they will receive what God has promised!
"Happy are those whose greatest desire is to do
        what God requires;
    God will satisfy them fully!
"Happy are those who are merciful to others;
    God will be merciful to them!
"Happy are the pure in heart;
    they will see God!
"Happy are those who work for peace;
    God will call them his children!
"Happy are those who are persecuted because they
        do what God requires;
        The Kingdom of heaven belongs to them!"
        —*Matthew 5:3-10*

1

Blessed Are the Poor in Spirit

How blest are those who know their need of God; the kingdom of Heaven is theirs. (NEB)

The Ten Commandments form the framework for the Mosaic Law and our ethical codes. The Beatitudes, likewise, serve as an outline of Jesus' teachings. In one way or another, everything Jesus says fits their framework.

Yet the Beatitudes do more than outline Jesus' theology. These "to be attitudes" remind us that salvation in Christ is a process that leads us from fearing frustration and failure to experiencing serenity and acceptance.

Perhaps the most unsettling thing about the Beatitudes is that they turn all of our perceptions upside down. They applaud the very attributes we grew up believing were signs of spiritual and moral weakness. This is especially true of the first beatitude.

Jesus sets out on the path to abundant living by showing us how to love and accept ourselves. The first step involves coming to terms with our inherent neediness and spiritual poverty. Jesus not only gives us permission to have needs. Jesus *blesses* our neediness.

Accepting Our Limitations

It's difficult to take on the challenges each day brings when we're afraid to make mistakes. Realizing it's all right to be spiritually and emotionally poor takes the shame out of being needy. It opens us to embrace life as it is, not as we want it to be. It places us where God can truly help us.

We can get emotionally mixed up when we equate selfishness with self-love. This is because selfishness is actually the opposite of self-love. Selfishness and self-hatred are what truly go hand in hand.

Feeling inadequate and unlovable makes us become obsessed with meeting our own needs. We try to grab things for ourselves. Convinced no one cares about us, we demand attention and insist on having our own way.

When, however, we accept and value ourselves, we open ourselves to trust others. Accepting the reality of a situation doesn't mean we quit trying to change. It means we stop trying to make things fit our wishes and expectations.

Nothing changed in our family as long as we denied the reality of our children's drug addiction. When we accepted their addiction as real, we were no longer so frustrated. Acceptance freed us to focus on the things we could change. It helped us view things from a different view point. It gave us choices and options.

Surrender goes a step beyond acceptance. Surrender lets us seek God's will. It frees us to give up our self-limiting beliefs and attitudes. Asking God to solve a specific problem is a specific way to pray, "*My* will be done." Few of us really know what we want, let alone what's best for us. So asking God to do things our way is risky. Surrender frees us to sincerely pray, "*Thy* will be done."

Accepting our spiritual poverty means giving God control. When we limit our prayers to requests for guidance and courage to use the guidance when God gives it, life has a way of unfolding like a flower.

In the first beatitude, Jesus assures us we'll experience happiness when we accept our feelings of inadequacy without shame. This is because God never intended us to be self-sufficient. God made us to need God and others.

Being "poor in spirit" presents us with a paradox. Only complete surrender to our situation and our innate powerlessness empowers us. Only when we admit their absence do we find the hope and resources we seek. Allowing ourselves to be needy, to have problems, to hurt and suffer, opens the way to change.

AA, Al-Anon, and other Twelve Step Programs restate the first beatitude in their first three steps. We

• admitted that we were powerless over (name of

the specific problem) and that our lives had become unmanageable.

• came to believe that a Power greater than ourselves can restore us to sanity.

• made a decision to turn our will and our lives over to the care of God as we understood him.

In his book, *Becoming a New Person: Twelve Steps for Christians,* Philip St. Romain rephrases the first step to read, "We admit that we cannot realize our fullest human potential by living a life of selfishness." That wording makes a lot of sense, since most problems stem from selfishness.

Sin as Addiction

Sin is an addiction to selfishness. An addict is one who has so yielded to a habit, substance, or interest that it becomes all-consuming. Addicts are often described as being obsessive-compulsive. A substance, interest, or practice (such as alcohol, smoking, drugs, a sport, work, selfishness, or religion) takes over. The individual loses control over choices and responses. The desire for the addictive substance or activity becomes total. It becomes what the apostle Paul calls "slavery."

Recovery begins when we accept that this compulsion will never completely go away. For the rest of our lives we'll need to keep learning how to live without what we think we need to be happy. Diabetics dare never forget they're diabetic and need to take insulin and follow a diet. Like them, we dare never forget we're sinners. We're flawed, broken, needy persons, even when things go well.

It's been helpful to see my spiritual salvation this way. Since I'll never be free of my sinful tendencies, I'll never outgrow my need for God's help. I'll always need the insights and support I gain by going to church and reading the Bible.

Learning from Life's Lessons

Because of our family experience with addictions, I no longer feel my role as a parent or pastor gives me the right to impose my faith or beliefs on others. Nor do I feel it's my job to provide solutions for others.

When people come for help, I listen. When appropriate, I share my faith and offer them the hope I've found. I tell them that when life seemed most hopeless, God turned our pain and failure into an opportunity for growth. I give them permission to struggle. I trust them to find their own answers.

Our battle with addiction has broken, humbled, and enriched me. It has taught me I'm not the person I thought I was. My life isn't blame-free, nor do I have answers for myself, let alone for others. Like everyone else, I'm selfish and sinful. My only hope lies in each day handing my life over to God's care and guidance, so I can grow in understanding and grace.

"Blessed are the spiritually impoverished" speaks to me of an ongoing awareness that never changes. We remain spiritually poor even as we mature and grow, stop nagging, control our eating compulsions, quit smoking, reconcile with our spouse, learn to control our temper, recover from our divorce. Even accepting Christ as Lord and Savior doesn't rescue us from such poverty.

Instead, we live abundantly precisely to the extent we stay in touch with our continuing neediness, doubts, fears, insecurities, and emptiness.

Being "poor in spirit' means letting go and letting God. It means facing our self-centeredness. It means facing the ways we insist that life and our loved ones conform to our needs, wants, and expectations. It means admitting that no matter how well things are going or how well we function, we never stop needing God.

Each Day a New Beginning

The first beatitude reminds us that each day is a gift. Each new day is a reprieve. God doesn't give us a permanent fix when we go to God for help. God gives us what we need for that particular day or situation. Each day, as we turn to God for power and guidance, we allow God to respond to our needs in ways that are best for us.

We'll always be powerless to change many things that happen. Try as we will, we can't control other people. I can accept such limitations now that I understand my happiness and worth aren't dependent on what others do or on my being problem free.

Our struggles with addiction have taught me God's ways and solutions are often not mine. Serenity flows from trusting God's ways. The first beatitude affirms that running the world is God's job, not ours. All God asks is that we admit and embrace our sinfulness without shame. Once we face our neediness and inner poverty we can let go and let God give us what we need.

Growing spiritually (and for me that's come to mean being grateful, happy, and functional in spite of pain) is like taking a trip. We can't get where we want to go until we acknowledge our starting point.

When my husband and I finally started going to FA meetings, we acknowledged we were workaholics (seen as a good thing in the church). We admitted our children were into drugs and alcohol (seen as a bad thing in the church). Then we started feeling less hopeless. Once we could admit we were powerless over the diseases destroying our lives, we miraculously improved.

But the minute we forget these compulsions will always be a part of our lives, we quickly fall back into the old patterns. The spiral starts again. Jesus told a parable about cleaning the demon out of the house only to have six more come to take its place. He knew what he was talking about. That's exactly what happens with addictions and other dependencies.

Denial: Taking Over from God

If we're to live rich and abundant lives in spite of unsolved problems, we have to give God control. We have to acknowledge and respect the power and nature of selfishness and sin.

In the creation story, God forbade Adam and Eve to eat of the fruit of the tree of the knowledge of good and evil. The knowledge the fruit represents wasn't harmful in and of itself. The problem was that Adam and Eve weren't ready to discern and use such knowledge.

Thus the tree's fruit made all people defensive, egocentric, and arrogant. It made us people who deny our needs and mortality.

"Blessed are the poor in spirit" reminds us we can't be happy when we take on more than we can handle. We have emotional, spiritual, and physical limitations. God didn't create us to live apart from divine support.

Things go haywire when we cut God out of our daily lives by putting God in a box marked "Sunday" and "spiritual matters."

Most of us don't carry the "I am god" bit so far that we cheat, steal, kill, knock others around, and sexually use others for our own selfish pleasure. At least, I hope we don't. But we do play god every day of our lives. That's what being self-centered is all about—placing ourselves at the center of the universe.

I learned the hard way the destructive power of my selfish need to protect my children from pain, to be needed, to look good, to be a supermom, to prove my value by serving and pastoring. I learned this kept them and others in my church from assuming responsibility for their own choices and actions. Unfortunately, my self-centered need to look important contributed in many ways to our struggles with addiction.

"Blessed are you when you can acknowledge your spiritual and emotional poverty" offers a wholesome starting point. With those wonderful affirming words, Jesus gives us permission to value ourselves just as we are . . . even though we may be flawed, broken, uptight, vulnerable, scarred, scared, defensive.

"You'll feel so much better when you stop denying what's really going on and accept your limitations," says Jesus. "Face your problems. Confront the demons that destroy you. Acknowledge your poverty. Allow me to walk with you."

The problem, you see, isn't that we're overweight, work too much, or addicted. It isn't that we have a violent temper, we get depressed, gamble. It isn't that we overprotect our children, nor that we cheat on our income tax, are homosexual, are perfectionists.

The problem is that we lie to ourselves and others. We pretend we're different than we really are. Because we live a lie, we die inside a little every day. Our lives get crazier and crazier. Our pain squeezes so tight we have a heart attack. We find ourselves struggling with cancer, diabetes, hypertension. We become asmatic, depressed, sexually dysfunctional, abusive.

We can't find happiness and meaning in our lives if we're afraid to admit we're unhappy. We can't have our needs met if we deny we have needs. As long as we pretend things are just fine, as long as we deny what's really going on, we can't—and God won't—do anything. In that sense, denial is the unforgivable sin. It places us outside the realm of God's redemption.

Finding the Power in Powerlessness

Learning to laugh at ourselves helps us stay humble and centered. One way I've learned to stay honest without becoming a complainer is to use the Program definition of the word *fine*. FINE stands for Frustrated, Insecure, Neurotic, and Emotional, or—poor in spirit!

Now when I feel shaky and don't want to lie but am also reluctant to dump my dirty laundry in public, I laugh. I tell people "I'm just fine!"

"To be congratulated are those who realize that they are absolutely destitute without God and they come to trust him completely," is the way Richard Milham translates the first beatitude in his book, *Like It Is Today*. I like that translation.

Accepting our neediness and character defects empowers us. That's the miracle of grace. It plugs us into the divine energy source. It enables us to change in God directed ways.

The great insight of the first beatitude is this: every problem and need carries with it a gift. Every failure points us toward God, connecting us to the one who gives life meaning. The curse brings a blessing. God, you see, gives us exactly what we need—be that the problem or the solution!

Oh God, thank you that I can be Christ-centered and peace-filled no matter what is going on around me. Thank you for every moment of every day. With you, each day is a new beginning. Each moment is a new opportunity to touch the fears and worries that tie me to the past, tempt me to blame others, and cut me off from you. With your help I'll see life's troubles as gifts, not curses. I'll work at accepting my limitations and brokenness. Remind me that difficulty opens me to your care and guidance, and my neediness is the very thing that draws me to you. Amen.

2

Blessed Are They That Mourn

How blest are the sorrowful;
they shall find consolation. (NEB)

Spiritual growth takes time; it's like laying a brick wall. We start building at the bottom before we put on the top layers. Jesus doesn't call us to instant maturity or spiritual perfection. He knew change occurs slowly. The Beatitudes provide Jesus' systematic travel plan for our faith pilgrimage.

While we move forward based on what we've already learned, we often have to stop and retrace our steps. We begin each day admitting our selfishness and our pull toward insane behavior (insanity being our tendency to repeat destructive or negative patterns). As we take that first step, something opens inside, allowing us to touch our feelings.

Because of Christ, we can stop pretending things are better than they are. We can repent—change direction. Christ's death and resurrection frees us to face the fears and worries that so easily bind us to the past or tempt us to blame others.

Fighting Our Feelings

Jesus tells us to pray specifically, to name our needs and pains. That's where the second beatitude comes in. All of us fear our emotions. Feelings can be strong enough to overwhelm us. So instead of dealing with our pain, anger, or jealousy, we stuff them away.

Even though tucked safely out of sight, the feelings don't go away. Hidden and unresolved, they shape our responses. Then, not knowing why we do things, we make excuses for ourselves or blame others. We rationalize and defend behaviors that make us uncomfortable. We feel sad and depressed without knowing why. We get angry for no clear reason.

The first beatitude says, "Admit your pain and need" The second beatitude says, "It's good to feel your pain." The first beatitude calls us to intimate relationship with God. The second calls us to intimate relationship with ourselves.

Mourning means feeling our sorrow, pain, and regret. Mourning reminds us our inner self is damaged. But sorrow, when allowed to do its job, rallies the forces of healing on behalf of our bleeding souls. By helping the pus of self-pity drain away, grieving lances our emotional wounds.

For what should we grieve? The death of a loved one. Poor health. A broken marriage. Alienation from parents. A straying child. A crippling accident. Disappointments and difficulties at work. Cutting remarks. Moving to a new area. Broken dreams. Shattered hopes.

Learning to Live with the Past

All of us have a hard time facing "the bad" in ourselves. We'll go to any length to avoid facing character defects. Most fights, differences, divorces, or splits come because we're unwilling to face our mistakes and misjudgments, not because of what others did!

Many of our current problems are carry-overs from childhood. Growing up in dysfunctional families, we didn't receive the love, affirmation, and relational skills we needed to be confident and self-assured. We didn't learn how to deal with problems or resolve conflicts. Unhappy and insecure, we blamed ourselves for what went wrong.

Feelings and patterns of behavior learned in childhood shape our self-perceptions and behavior as adults. Unless relived, understood, and reinterpreted, these self-limiting patterns set us on a collision course with life.

Because we bury our feelings of worthlessness and inadequacy so deeply, we don't realize they keep us from achieving our goals. Convinced we're unworthy of happiness or success, we create situations where we fail.

Human beings have two basic emotional needs. We need to love and be loved. And we need to feel useful. If, as children, we didn't receive the love we needed (from parents who were themselves damaged and hurting), we may go through life emotionally crippled. While we can never go back and recover our lost childhood we don't need to let the past limit us.

This is precisely the situation Jesus addresses when he says, "Happy are those who can grieve— who can touch their deepest pain and emotions— for they shall find comfort."

We can face our pain and grieve our broken selves. Or we can deny the pain and allow it to go on distorting our lives.

We can forgive our parents and grieve with and for them, because they were also victims of life. Or we can blame them and harbor resentments that keep on poisoning us.

We end up with two basic choices. We can choose the pain that comes with growing and changing. Or we can choose the pain that comes from refusing to grow and change.

Grieving hurts, but denial finally hurts more. The feelings we send underground by ignoring them fester away. They influence every decision and response we make. And by burying them we give them far more power to control our actions and lives than if we allowed ourselves to cry and grieve!

Until we face and accept our wounds, we can't find comfort, strength, or healing. We can't find better ways to respond or act. We can't experience the love, joy, and serenity we long for and deserve—no matter who we are or what we've done.

When we shut away our pain, we shut away our positive feelings as well. True, things may seem better when we don't consciously feel the hurt, but that's an illusion. Anytime we suppress something, life flattens out.

The second step of AA parallels the second beatitude. The second step states, "[We] came to accept that a Power greater than ourselves could restore us to sanity."

Assurance that God can restore us to health and sanity is important because the grieving experience can be hellish! Openness to rage, hurt, and loss can make us feel as if we're literally losing our mind. Touching our shadow selves disorients and frightens us.

Most of us grew up believing it's wrong to respond passionately to life, especially when rage or hate drives our passion. Many of us need permission to feel and express our varied feelings. We need to know that it is not only safe and acceptable but important to our spiritual and emotional welfare. Jesus gives us that permission when he says, "Blessed are they that mourn."

Jesus also knew we usually need a trusted person to listen and affirm us, especially when we're in the process of accepting and disarming our pain. This is one reason the Twelve Step Programs stress the Fifth Step. "[We] admitted to God, to ourselves, and to another human being the exact nature of our wrongs." Daring to share the confusion and dark secrets that eat at our being helps us experience love as a reality.

Jesus tells us we're blessed as we allow ourselves to feel deeply, whether those feelings seem logical or not. When we let ourselves feel what we *really* feel, not what we're *supposed* to feel, things change. Something deep within is energized. We find new ways to understand and respond. God restores us to sanity by helping us reinterpret past events and see situations from a different viewpoint.

Grieving is the second step in our spiritual journey because grief is a proper response to craziness and chaos. Grief gets us back on track. It frees us to see through new eyes, God's eyes.

When we grieve, we start by feeling helpless and hopeless. But as we embrace our pain, the miracle of healing begins. As we look for God's gift and promise hidden in the midst of pain, we literally grieve our way into hope.

Turning Tragedy into Triumph

It wasn't until we faced how badly our family situation had degenerated that we could acknowledge how crazy we had all become. But real change began for me the day I finally allowed myself to weep.

I wept for my fantasy of the perfect Christian family and love's power to cross racial and cultural lines. I wept because I wasn't the perfect mother. I wept because my marriage was coming apart. I wept because my children were alcoholics and alienated from me. I wept because I was literally going crazy. I wept because I realized just how weak I was.

But after that two-day crying jag came peace of mind and heart. Washed clean by tears, I could accept myself, my children, and my husband. I could face what we each were—beautiful though broken children of God.

It wasn't until I could let go of that fantasy and its power over me that God could give it back to me in altered form. And give it back God has. I'm discovering God has given us the task of modeling Christian family life, after all.

But now, we don't look like the Brady Bunch, whose children never made serious mistakes, ran away, or get arrested. Now God has called us to show others how to rise above heartbreak and failure. Through our story, they can see that God is indeed a loving and forgiving God who never gives up.

Depression: Anger Turned Inward

Many of us struggle with depression. Some depression is organic in nature. It stems from physiological and chemical malfunctions. But much depression stems from buried and denied feelings. We turn our pain and anger inward, focusing it on ourselves, punishing ourselves. We think it's our fault when we can't make others do what we want them to do. We feel as if we've failed when we can't protect our loved ones from harm or poor choices.

Some of us get so depressed when we fail that we use our depression as a buffer against the pain. We become so sad we can't feel anything—joy *or* pain. Grief reconnects us with our pain and allows us to start anew.

Following a particularly painful counseling session some years ago, I had a vision of myself as a nesting toy. The outer layers were the competent, efficient, talented parts of me. But each successive layer became less and less competent. At the very center was hidden this terrified, hunch-backed little urchin. Her pain controlled all the other me's! That little creature stopped running my life only as I learned to comfort, nurture, and love her instead of hiding her away.

Taking Our Cues from Christ

In the Beatitudes Jesus shows us the process that moves us toward abundant life. It's a process that calls us to embrace life's darkness and shadows. Such embrace releases the divine light that transforms pain. While we can't deny evil, we can overcome it with love.

On the night of Jesus' betrayal, Jesus grieved for what had already happened, as well as for what lay ahead. He begged God to spare him additional suffering. Yet as he struggled with his fear and grief, he found not just comfort but strength to face what lay ahead. Out of his willingness to face and embrace his pain, Jesus experienced new life, for our sake as well as his own.

The first beatitude tells us to claim our birthright as God's child by affirming our connections with our heavenly Father. The second beatitude asks us to face our fragility on an even deeper level. In this step we not only acknowledge our fallibility and our brokenness. We embrace it. We grieve for all our might-have-beens. We confess we do get sick. We do get angry. We do hurt each other. We do make mistakes, we do fail, we do grow old. And we do die.

Jesus was harder on those who were dishonest and pretentious than on those who openly sinned, because hypocrisy involves denial. Grief is a way to come to terms with the truth about life. It restores us to sanity. It helps us accept ourselves for who and what we are. "Blessed are they that mourn, for they shall be comforted" is the promise and permission that we can indeed grieve our way into hope and healing. As the psalmist said, "Tears may flow in the night, but joy comes in the morning."

"Blessed, happy, enviable, on the path to spiritual prosperity (joy in God's favor and salvation, regardless of outward conditions) are they who feel their pain. For they will find the comfort strength, and healing they seek."

> *O Lord, giver of life, hear my prayer.*
> *Beyond the absence, your presence*
> *Beyond the pain, healing*
> *Beyond the brokenness, wholeness*
> *Beyond the anger, peace*
> *Beyond the hurting, forgiveness*
> *Beyond the grief, comfort*
> *Beyond the silence, your word*
> *And in that Word, understanding*
> *And in the understanding, love*
> *Love and new beginnings.*
> *O Lord, be with me as I grieve my way*
> *into hope.*
> *Amen.*

3

Blessed Are the Meek

Blessed are the meek for they shall inherit the earth. (King James)

Harnessing Our Spiritual Horsepower

This beatitude confuses many of us. The words *meek* or *humble* conjure up meanings that stress our already shaky self-concepts. Over the years we've equated meekness with being mousy and humility with self-negation. But Jesus didn't make that mistake. For Jesus humility meant being able to love ourselves so we could love our neighbors. Jesus linked humility with quiet self-confidence. This caused others to say of him, "He speaks with authority."

Words are never emotion-free, because words reflect our experiences. When we deal with words like *sin, meek,* and *humble*, it's often difficult to find proper synonyms. Over the years, the faith community has developed its own language, even though the meanings of specific words may have changed with time.

The word *humble* stems from the Latin word *humas*, meaning *earth*. Humble people are meek, unassuming, unpretentious. They're not easily angered or quick to resent. They're aware of their defects and shortcomings.

Meek is a synonym of *humble*, and the more common choice for translators even though the meaning has shifted over the years. Originally a verb and not a noun, it described the process used to train and domesticate animals. That concept has profound implications for us.

"Meeked" animals include magnificent Lichstenstein horses from Vienna, Austria; sheep dogs working the flock; seeing-eye dogs helping blind masters. This is precisely the type of God-person relationship Jesus means when he says, "Blessed are the meek."

When we accept our powerlessness and need, God can meek us. God can teach us the skills we need to live abundantly. Becoming meeked implies becoming responsible—able to respond. It means opening ourselves to direction from the God who ultimately controls our lives.

Looking back, I see my trying experiences as times of meeking. Being a slow learner, I repeated some mistakes again and again. I resisted accepting our family addictions, as well as several surgeries and slow recoveries. When I recall them, I now see myself as a wild horse captured by the divine cowpoke. I bucked and fought before finally cooperating.

As I began to use my energy to work with instead of bucking God, I discovered being meeked didn't make me less spirited. It enhanced my zest for life instead.

God doesn't meek us to destroy us. God meeks us to prepare us for abundant living. God meeks us so we can be useful and can better enjoy life. God meeks us so we can discover how to tap into a power source greater than we've ever known!

Moving to Specifics

Becoming meeked and humbled is so important that seven of the Twelve Steps are specifically devoted to it. When we are meeked we have

- made a searching and fearless moral inventory of ourselves.
- admitted to God, to ourselves, and to another human being the exact nature of our wrongs.
- become entirely ready to have God remove all of these defects of character.
- humbly asked him to remove all our shortcomings.

These steps remind me of Psalm 131, which I memorized and which has helped me in my struggle with humility and meeking.

Lord, I have given up my pride
and turned away from my arrogance.
I am not concerned with great matters
or with subjects too difficult for me.
Instead, I am content and at peace.
As a child lies quietly in its mother's arms,

so my heart is quiet within me.
Israel, trust in the Lord now and forever!

Humility as Surrender

Jesus was a good psychologist. He knew people. He didn't paint the meeking process as negative— though he didn't lie about its pain, either. He pointed out that humility would lead to our inheriting the earth. Humility would place us in positions of trust, power, and influence.

The doors of life do open to those who are truly humble, tolerant, and unpretentious. We know we open our own door to such people. We like to work with people who don't get angry or hold grudges. Who aren't judgmental or critical. Who are willing to look at themselves and their role in a problem as well as the role others play.

Jesus also refrained from those two terrible words that rob us of freedom and choice, *should* and *must*. Jesus didn't tell us we must not be arrogant. He instead invited us to let go of arrogance by pointing out that such surrender makes us feel whole and healthy.

One of the devotional books I frequently use is *One Day at a Time in Al-Anon*. It says that

> True humility does not mean to seek surrender to an ugly destructive way of life. It means surrender to God's will which is quite a different thing. Humility prepares us for the realization of God's will for us; it shows us the benefits we gain from doing away with self-will. We finally understand how this self-will has actually contributed to our distress.

The attitude of humility confers dignity and grace on us; it shows us the benefits we gain from doing away with self-will. . . . [It] strengthens us to take intelligent spiritual action in solving our problems. (page 61)

Humility and Anger

As I said earlier, the humble person isn't riddled with anger and resentment. But many of us *are* angry and resentful.

Living with alcoholic children made *me* angry and confused. I loved my children. I also hated them. Oh how I resented what they were doing to us all! Every night I went to bed terrified that something awful would happen. Every morning I awoke afraid to face the day. Sometimes the pain, fear, and chaos got so bad I wished they'd die. That would end the nightmare. Then I'd sink into a pit of self-loathing for thinking such thoughts.

Anger and resentment do terrible things to us. We wear ourselves out when we put all our energy into being angry and nursing grudges instead of more constructive responses. The third beatitude could be paraphrased, "Happy are those who don't react to criticism, frustration, or difficult situations with anger or resentment. For they will receive the blessings God has promised."

Surprisingly enough, anger is a secondary emotion. While very powerful, it's secondary in the sense that it's a response to something. It's a defense mechanism. It protects us from more basic feelings we fear experiencing directly.

When my children came home high or stoned I

was frantic with worry. I was terrified their drug use would hurt or finally kill them. But they rarely saw my concern. What they saw was my anger.

When we started going to FA I learned more constructive responses. FA offered me a spiritual response to fear and anxiety. Instead of worrying or seething with resentment, I prayed The Serenity Prayer or studied the Twelve Steps.

At night when I'd lie awake sick with worry, I'd picture my troubled children surrounded by a white light representing God's love and protection. Instead of tossing and turning I'd try to guess where they might be, then imagine that white light leaving my heart. It would travel down the road, around several bends, turning at the crossroads until it found them and enveloped them with love and concern.

Having turned them over to God and knowing God was caring for them, I could let go of my anger or fear, at least for the time being. I also learned to see their behaviors as symptoms of an illness, rather than as willful acts of disobedience.

Because anger is a secondary emotion preventing our confronting an underlying but hidden emotion, the apostle Paul is right when he says, "Don't let the sun go down on your anger." Putting off dealing with our anger makes it harder to find the underlying pain which drives it.

Giving God the Reins

"Blessed are the meek" is similar to the Third Step, which is to have "made a decision to turn our will and our lives over to the care of God as we understand him." All I have to do to see the connection is remember how chaotic our lives were when our children were using drugs and alcohol! There was so much pain. We were always fighting, yelling, hurting each other. Our lives were unmanageable, out of control.

But now that we're turning our wills and lives over to God's care, we're no longer trying to make things happen a certain way. With God in charge, we're learning to talk to each other, to work together. Most of the wild scenes are gone. Sure, we still argue and disagree. But we now have a point of contact: we care about each other! We all have a sense of the God within and without.

The Twelve Steps and the Eight Beatitudes are helpful not just because they encapsulate great spiritual wisdom and direction in concise and understandable form. They're also helpful because they ease us toward greater health and maturity by breaking down the "meeking process" into steps we can handle. We can't change all our negative attitudes and behaviors at once. It's a process that goes like this:

We take a good hard look at ourselves and quit making excuses for our bad habits and attitudes.

We learn to *accept and value* our strengths and gifts.

Having faced those things we need to change to be happy and serene, we're ready to do something difficult. We're ready to *confess* our faults, not just to ourselves and God in the privacy of our "closet," but to someone we trust.

Having confessed the things we've avoided or denied for so long, both good and bad, we become ready to allow God to help us *change*.

Then we ask God to *meek* us, to remove our shortcomings, literally to change our personality in ways that pleases God. As this happens (and the process takes months and years) we're empowered to let go of our pride and to do two things.

First we *make a list of people we have hurt* and the ways we hurt them.

Then we actually *do something to make amends*, such as writing letters, going to see people, paying back debts, accepting responsibility, and using our talents.

Serenity: Why Meeking Is Worthwhile

The New English Bible uses the word *gentle* instead of *meek*. "How blest are those of a gentle spirit." I like that. I like realizing that the outcome of all those painful meeking and humbling experiences leads to my becoming gentle-spirited and serene.

Because serenity is such an important part of humility, the Twelve Step Programs use a prayer called The Serenity Prayer or the AA Prayer. Members are encouraged to memorize The Serenity Prayer and pray it when met with difficult situations or tempted to backslide.

I generally pray the shortened version. But I much prefer the longer version (sometimes attributed to Reinhold Neibuhr), for it puts into a few words all I long for in my relationship with my God and Savior.

God, grant me serenity to accept the things I cannot change, courage to change the things I can, and wisdom to know the difference. Living one day at a time, enjoying one moment at a time, accepting hardship as a pathway to peace. Taking, as Jesus did, this sinful world as it is, not as I would have it. Trusting that you will make all things right if I surrender to Your will, so that I may be reasonably happy in this life and supremely happy with you forever in the next. Amen.

—Traditionally ascribed
to Reinhold Niebuhr

4

Blessed Are They That Hunger and Thirst

Blessed and fortunate and happy and spiritually prosperous [that is, in that state in which the born-again child of God enjoys His favor and salvation] are those who hunger and thirst for righteousness [uprightness and right standing with God], for they shall be completely satisfied!" (AMP)

Inch by inch, step by step, day by day the Beatitudes lead us toward greater wholeness and spiritual health. Learning to let go and let God be in control frees us to grieve our losses, our mistakes, and our disappointments. As we touch what's really going on inside us, we become less defensive. We no longer interpret difficulties as punishments but as opportunities for growth.

Inch by inch, step by step, day by day, sometimes gracefully, sometimes awkwardly, sometimes kicking and screaming, sometimes slipping back and needing to start all over, we move into God's open future. But move we do.

Righteousness: More Than Rules

Many of us associate righteousness with following a set of carefully defined rules. But righteousness has more to do with honoring relationships than following rules. Righteousness involves being able to accept ourselves and others just as we are, not as we think we should be. Such acceptance is necessary for "right living," for it opens the way to change. It allows us to enjoy life and to trust in the face of pain.

Rules are important if we're to function in community. Rules and laws help create order by setting standards. Without such guidelines we wouldn't know what was expected of us. We wouldn't know what we could and couldn't do to be loved, safe, and sane.

The Ten Commandments form the basis for our legal and religious systems. They establish the perimeters of our social interactions. They're designed to give us the social structures we need to develop healthy relationships with God, self, and others. While worded in the negative, the Ten Commandments aren't so much a list of forbidden behaviors as positive guidelines for meaningful human interactions.

The fourth beatitude builds on the Ten Commandments and helps us in our search for God's will. Hungering and thirsting after righteousness forces us to examine our attitudes and behaviors. It causes us to ask the hard questions, to take a good look at ourselves.

Do we refrain from stealing because we know

stealing is wrong? Or because we are afraid of getting caught?

Are we polite because we care for others? Or because we want to make a good impression?

Do we go to church because we want to worship God? Or because it will make us look good?

Does generosity stir our giving? Or getting a tax deduction?

Do we vote for the person we think will govern well and be sensitive to the poor and needy? Or do we vote for the one who will make sure our business won't lose its tax loopholes?

"Blessed are those who hunger and thirst after righteousness" tells us to look at our basic motives. Being righteous involves taking a fearless moral inventory of ourselves and righting wrongs we've committed. It demands that we love ourselves, use our gifts, take risks, and reach out to others.

Guidelines for Right Living

Now Jesus roots his approach to righteousness in living by the spirit (looking at *motives* as well as *actions*) rather than the letter of the law (adopting a legalistic approach).

But Jesus knows we desperately need rules to help us in our daily interactions. Thus he makes us a promise. If we seek to do God's will, based on our best understanding of Jesus' guidelines for right living, our needs will be met. Our awareness of God's presence and reality will increase. "Set your mind on God's kingdom and his justice before everything else, and all the rest will come to you as well" (Matthew 6:33, NEB).

In the Sermon on the Mount, Jesus takes all the principles he addresses in the Beatitudes, breaks them down into understandable concepts, and illustrates how they work. I developed for my own use an outline of Matthew 5 through 7 which goes like this:

(1) Don't apologize for your faith, even when it differs from the norm. Be positive about your commitment to God. (5:14-16)

(2) Take the Scriptures seriously. They're "The Guide" to life. (5:17-20)

(3) Unresolved anger is destructive. Holding grudges, nursing resentments, calling people names, or putting them down, makes trouble for everyone, including yourself. Take the initiative in working toward resolution and reconciliation. (5:21-26)

(4) Lust abuses and devalues others, including yourself. It turns everyone into a sex object. Adultery violates existing relationships. (5:27-30)

(5) Don't use divorce as a cop-out when things get rough. Don't walk away from your problems or blame others for what goes wrong. Work on doing what you can to improve the situation because divorce radically changes things for everyone involved. (5:31-32)

(6) Be honest. Don't tell lies or embellish the truth. Your credibility depends on your honesty. In legal situations, as in any situation, simply tell the truth. Taking an oath doesn't guarantee honesty. (5:33-37)

(7) Don't try to get even when someone takes

advantage of you. Take control of the situation by cooperating instead of fighting back. The best way to respond when someone tries to humiliate you is to change the rules by not buying into their violence or greedy logic. Even if you can't keep them from doing hurtful things, you can refuse to let the situation humiliate or demean you. (5:38-42)

(8) Love your enemies. Hatred and vengeful behavior don't hurt their target. They destroy the one who hates! Love and forgiveness keep us aligned with God and open the way for change. (5:43-48)

(9) Respect the integrity and anonymity of the poor and needy. Don't give just to make yourself look good. We can make things worse when we help others for the wrong reasons. (6:1-4)

(10) Be wary of your attitude toward possessions and money. It's easy to make financial security and wealth an end in itself. Money has value in the kingdom as we use it to meet basic needs and to help others. (6:19-34)

(11) Let go and let God. To paraphrase the Serenity Prayer, accept what you can't change, and change the things you can. Life is too precious to waste time worrying. God will help us meet our basic needs. (6:25-31)

(12) Stop focusing on what others do. Change and improve yourself instead of criticizing and judging others. Working on yourself gives you credibility and the right to confront others when appropriate. (7:1-6)

(13) Be specific about your needs and concerns

when you pray. Avoid lofty generalizations. (7:7-11)

(14) Treat others fairly. Be consistent. Treat them the way you wish to be treated. (7:12)

(15) Accept that life is often difficult. Let go of your fantasy that righteous living should make things easier. (7:13)

(16) Be discerning. If you doubt another's motives or position, pay attention to what they do more than what they say. Religious talk comes cheap! (7:15-23)

(17) Place God at the center of everything you do. (8:23)

(18) Act on what you believe. Don't be afraid to take risks. It's okay to make mistakes when stepping out in faith. Trust leads to greater faith and trust. (7:23-26)

Getting Our Priorities Straight

In the Fourth Beatitude, Jesus reminds us our priorities are askew when we seek only to please people. God's the one we should please because putting God first affects all our other relationships —be they with spouse, children, family, friends, employer, church, or country. Seeking God's rather than our friends' approval is scary. Human approval is so tangible, so immediate. Divine approval is so elusive, so hidden.

For years I put our children's needs before my husband's and my own. The family suffered. Then I realized I had my priorities turned around. I'm first a child of God, then a wife, then a mother. Not only is that order important to the family, but it works for everything we do. We're first a child of God—*then* pastor, group leader, committee member.

Taking care of ourselves isn't selfish when we turn to God as primary source and resource. With our basic love and success needs met and our priorities clear, we can be there for others. We can love and affirm them even when they're less than lovable. We can give unstintingly of ourselves if we keep our focus on Christ.

AA's Tenth and Eleventh Steps sum up this particular beatitude well. We

- continued to take personal inventory and when we were wrong promptly admitted it.
- sought through prayer and meditation to improve our conscious contact with God as we understood him, praying only for knowledge of his will for us and the power to carry that out.

It's so tempting to separate spirituality from everyday living. "Happy are those whose hearts' desire is righteousness" confronts our tendency to segment our lives. Everything we do, think, feel, and say affects how we respond to ourselves, God, and others. Our children learned they have to follow the Twelve Step Program every day to stay sober and healthy. We Christians, similarly, must follow God's program every day to participate in the kingdom of God.

Priscilla Brandt tells a wonderful story about hungering and thirsting after righteousness in her book, *Two-Way Prayer.* A young man goes to his teacher and asks:

> "Tell me, sir, how can I get to know God?"
>
> The teacher took him out into a lake and told him to put his head under the water. As he did, the teacher held the student's head under the water with his hand. The student struggled and fought to come to the surface. Still the teacher held his head firmly. Finally in desperation the man gave one last gallant attempt to surface, and came sputtering and gasping for air. "What are your trying to do? I almost drowned! I couldn't get my breath!"
>
> The teacher said, "Tell me, what were you thinking about all of the time I held your head in the water?"
>
> "Only one thing, sir. All I could think of was 'I want air. . . . I need air. . . . I've got to have air or I'll die."
>
> "That's how badly you have to want God, and then you will know him!" the wise teacher replied.

"Happy are you when your greatest desire in life is to seek God's will and to please God, for when you do, you will be filled," Jesus tells us in this "to-be-attitude." We're to humble ourselves beneath God's mighty hand. Then, even if we can't understand God's leadings, we can rest in God's will and bask in God's peace.

When we want God so badly that we know something in us will die if we don't find God, God satisfies our longing. God fills us with his Holy Spirit. God sends the Helper, the Comforter, the one who can walk with us in our journey toward right living.

That's the promise that accompanies seeking righteousness.

> *Light of the world, light my way, for I would know and do your will. Illuminate my heart and mind, that I might see with your eyes, hear with your ears, speak with your words, think with your thoughts, and love as you love. Fill me with your spirit, O Lord, that others might be drawn to you and your way. Amen.*

5

Blessed Are the Merciful

*Happy are those who show mercy to others;
God will show mercy to them.*

The story of the good Samaritan is about mercy.
It dramatically illustrates the Fifth Beatitude.

This parable fascinates most of us. It answers that
basic question, "Who is my neighbor?" and in so
doing crosses racial and cultural lines. What really
fascinates us, however, is that it holds up a mirror
so we can see ourselves and our many personalities
and roles.

Our Many Selves

Each character in the parable of the good Samaritan represents a part of ourselves. We're never one
character all the time. Sometimes life beats us up
and leaves us nursing our wounds or dying by the
roadside. Other times we get so caught up in ourselves and what we have to do we either don't no-
tice or can't be bothered to help the hurting. Then
there are times we *are* willing and able to be there
for others.

Through this story, Jesus shows us our many selves. This helps move us beyond judgmentalism to empathy. Jesus tells the parable so we can let go of our self-limiting views and become the well-rounded people God wants us to be.

There's a saying in Twelve Step circles that goes, "If you keep doing what you're doing, you'll keep getting what you're getting." This suggests mercy is like a boomerang. If we send mercy out it will return to us.

"Blessed are the merciful" reminds us of the basic soundness of the Golden Rule, "Do unto others as you would have them do unto you." It also echoes the Great Commandment, "Love the Lord your God with your heart, soul, and mind, and your neighbor as yourself" (Luke 10:27). What we give is what we get. It's as simple as that!

The Twelve Steps gently sidestep judgment. They invite us to grow one step at a time without insisting we be at a different place in our journey than we're ready for. So also do the Beatitudes lead us gently but firmly forward in our spiritual, emotional, and relational journey through life. Step by step they ease us over one hurdle after another. They help us build on both our positive and negative experiences, so we can grow "in wisdom and stature, and in favor with God and men" (Luke 2:52).

Before we examine further the implications of this beatitude, let's take a minute to recap the steps which have brought us thus far.

(1) Blessed are the poor in spirit. . . . Admit your selfishness, your emptiness, your inner poverty.

(2) Blessed are they who mourn. . . . Face your pain and loss, grieve for your brokenness and disappointments.

(3) Blessed are the meeked. . . . Allow yourself to be opened, taught, humbled, and forgiven.

(4) Blessed are they who hunger and thirst after righteousness. . . . Reach for the good in life. Turn your will and life over to the care of God.

(5) Blessed are the merciful. . . . Knowing yourself as loved and valued in spite of your failures and shortcomings, reach out to others and offer them chances to begin anew. Don't judge others!

Pain Is Inevitable

Unless we know what it's like to be beaten up and broken by life, and how it feels when those we love and trust betray us, we'll never grasp the revolutionary nature of the Jesus story. Jesus' death and resurrection don't make sense apart from the betrayals that motivated them.

Some years ago I attended a retreat at the Church of the Savior. Elizabeth O'Connor spoke to our group about forgiveness. She told of being betrayed by a friend. As she reflected on that experience, she made the observation that it's the context of betrayal and pain that gives the crucifixion and resurrection meaning.

Jesus' role as Savior emerged from his struggle to rise above the devastating hurt and disappointment he felt when trusted ones betrayed him. It was in the context of these real-life situations that he faced his own humanity and divinity.

Like us, Jesus was tempted. Like us, he felt resentments. Like us, he longed for revenge, power, and control. But he confronted the true nature of his feelings. He used them to forge new and divinely inspired responses. He became our Savior as he chose alternative behaviors and responses so revolutionary and life-changing they changed world history!

We're often tempted to view Jesus as above such human emotions as anger, hatred, and pain. Yet his life and teachings take on the ring of authority precisely because they are rooted in human experience. In the brief accounts the Bible records, we see Jesus grappling with the pain he felt when his family, friends, and followers repeatedly disappointed him.

He even, it seems, experienced that sense of ultimate abandonment. During his crucifixion he cried out in anguish and despair, "My God, my God, why have you forsaken me?"

"Blessed are they who mourn" gives us permission to feel every emotion. There are no right or wrong, good or bad feelings. Feelings just are. What we do with them, how we choose to act on them, is what counts.

Through "Blessed are the merciful," Jesus tells us how to respond to betrayal and pain without allowing evil and suffering to defeat us. The beatitude takes us beyond feelings to constructive action. It calls us not only to permit others to be fallible. It calls us to give them support, acceptance, and opportunities to change and start over.

Disappointments, betrayals, and unanticipated difficulties are part of life. In Twelve Step circles we have a saying: "Pain is inevitable, but suffering is optional." Jesus showed that truth in his own life. No matter how good or faithful we are, pain will find us. It's part of life.

Since we'll inevitably be wounded, pain isn't the issue. How we respond to pain is the issue. Realizing that we impose much of our suffering on ourselves by our response to it allows us to choose better responses.

Jesus showed us how to handle pain without becoming bitter, critical, judgmental, legalistic, or suspicious. He showed us how to move beyond the major cause of most of our suffering—our own attitudes. Jesus was in harmony with his Parent's will for him. This gave him insight to choose when to take on the suffering of others and when to let them suffer the results of their own actions.

Jesus thus points us toward a way of life that helps us embrace pain without being crushed by it. He also shows us how we can be thankful and joyful even when everything seems to be going wrong. Central to the strategy Jesus modeled and teaches us is mercy. Mercy for ourselves as well as for others!

Learning to Forgive Ourselves

Many of us are harder on ourselves than others. Our betrayal of ourselves often pains us more than being betrayed by others.

Jesus calls us to be merciful to ourselves as well

as others, instead of being critical, apathetic, or judgmental.

When we can see ourselves mirrored in the different characters in the parable of the good Samaritan, we can avoid the deadly traps of judging and criticizing. We can stop taking inventory of people's faults and blaming them. We can stop making lists and checking them twice. We can instead forgive.

We can be open, loving, and merciful without lowering our ethical standards. We, after all, make mistakes. Instead of reacting defensively or thoughtlessly when hurtful things happen, we can choose our response. This gives us a better grip on life and its problems. Because we become merciful through self-knowledge and self-acceptance, steps four through ten of the Twelve Steps help us develop the self-knowledge that leads to mercy. We

(4) made a searching and fearless moral inventory of ourselves.

(5) admitted to God, ourselves, and another human being the exact nature of our wrongs.

(6) were entirely ready to have God remove all of these defects of character.

(7) humbly asked him to remove our shortcomings.

(8) made a list of all persons we have harmed and became ready to make amends to them all.

(9) made direct amends to such people whenever possible, except when to do so would injure them or others.

(10) continued to take personal inventory and when we were wrong promptly admitted it.

It would be nice if we could change just by reading the steps or the Beatitudes. However, we have to work the steps by doing what they say. That's the hard part.

Avoiding the Blaming Game

When we're hurting and feeling insecure, we tend to protect ourselves by focusing on someone else's faults. It's easier to see how others hurt themselves with their fantasies, destructive life commandments, and unrealistic expectations than to acknowledge those tendencies in ourselves. Yet Jesus teaches us we can move forward in our journey of faith when we look at ourselves and change what needs changing.

We grow only as we let go of our anger, resentment, and pain, even when such feelings are justified. Such feelings, unfaced, are what hold us back—not what others do! We grow when we stop excusing ourselves or blaming others and allow God to meek us into joyous and creative mercy.

Mercy can't exist apart from forgiveness. In the parable of the good Samaritan, Jesus paints a picture of good and upright people threatened by the injured man and his situation. The victims of our society likewise threaten us. When we find it hard to respond to others it's because we're reacting to our own fears, not to what the other is doing. Let me illustrate.

After a life-threatening illness I found it hard to go back to my chaplaincy work at the nursing home. I not only avoided those who were dying, I considered resigning.

When my son is late I get upset because *I'm* often late.

Accounts of child abuse inflame me partly because the violence I know lurks within me frightens me.

When we overreact to what someone is saying or doing, we're often reacting to that same tendency or characteristic in ourselves.

In one Fourth Step work sheet I found the following description of the seven deadly sins, which the Twelve Step Program calls "character defects." This breakdown of sins into fears helped me understand myself and my own reactions. I keep a copy on my refrigerator to remind me that the only solution to my fear is admitting my powerlessness and inner poverty.

> Pride is a fear of the truth.
> Greed is a fear of being in need.
> Lust is a fear of rejection.
> Anger is a fear of being hurt, disappointed, etc.
> Gluttony is a fear of being in want.
> Envy is a fear of accepting ourselves as we are.
> Laziness is a fear of responsibility.

We Can't Change Others

Forgiveness, while difficult, is such a gift because we often judge others without thinking, without "walking a mile in their moccasins," as a native American saying goes. So we back ourselves into a corner and end up reacting to our own fears instead of responding to the other's situation or need.

Then we end up being the one needing forgiveness, because we've lapsed into judgmentalism. Mercy becomes ours for the giving and taking as we perceive that we can't change others but only ourselves.

Working on ourselves goes a long way toward making a bad situation better. When my husband and I began attending FA meetings, we were encouraged to take the focus off our addicts and put it on ourselves. I couldn't see how that would help. After all, I wasn't the one using alcohol. Yet as I began changing some attitudes and behaviors, (like my yelling and crying) I discovered that changing myself worked!

Concentrating on what we were doing called my children into accountability without judging or condemning them. My husband and I developed new responses. We stepped back from blaming and self-destructive behaviors. This offered our children hope and reassurance. It suggested that if we could change, they could too.

This is why the focus of any Twelve Step Program is working on oneself and letting others be as good or bad as they choose. By changing ourselves we open the doors to a new relationship with the person we've feared or resented.

Jesus says, "Judge not, that you be not judged" (Matthew 7:1). Following this train of thought to its logical conclusion, the person we must first forgive is ourself. We judge others because we have not forgiven ourselves. Once we do forgive ourselves, we can cut the spiral of judgment, neither judging nor being judged but giving and receiving mercy.

Forgiveness: God's Alternative

Since acts of betrayal are so much part of everyday life, we have to find ways to deal with and move beyond them. Our happiness depends on our willingness to let go of our hurts, difficult though that may be.

Jesus forgave those who hurt him as he hung on the cross. And he did so not just for their sakes but his own. He knew that inability to forgive hurts us far more than the one we refuse to forgive. He knew if he clung to fear and resentment, all he believed and knew about himself and God would be lost.

He also knew he couldn't forgive by himself. He needed God's help. He had to acknowledge his powerlessness to rise above his pain apart from God.

"Blessed are the merciful" reminds us we must make peace with ourselves before we can make peace with others. Mercy means that even if we don't know why someone does what they do, for our own sakes—if not theirs—we must accept them as they are. Outside of forgiveness, we remain forever nailed to the painful crosses of our past.

God's plan for our salvation depended on Jesus' ability to forgive. Jesus could have cursed his betrayers. He could have rejected his disciples for their cowardice and failure as he had every right to do. He could have resorted to violence and retribution. But then there would be no Jesus for us today. No Savior, no resurrection, no eternal life.

But Jesus did forgive. When on the cross he forgave those who hurt and betrayed him, he freed his divinity to shine forth. So also does the Holy Spirit help our new natures shine forth when we forgive those who hurt and betray us.

The tragedy of Judas's life is not that he betrayed Jesus but that he yielded to despair. It's that he was unable to forgive himself and to wait long enough to see the miracle God had in store for him!

Yet who can condemn Judas for his suicide? Forgiveness isn't the norm. It's an unexpected, mysterious, unmerited gift from the merciful, whose own pain and suffering has taught them to anoint failure with forgiveness.

In the Lord's Prayer, Jesus tells us to forgive others or not expect forgiveness for ourselves. He reminds us to bypass judging others so we won't be judged. As we accept ourselves as flawed, capable of great evil, we can accept the shortcomings of others. We can call forth a better life in ourselves and in them. As we accept our faults we name and confront the demons that lie within us so we can tame them.

Therein lies the power of AA and other Twelve Step Programs. Seeing ourselves in each other reminds us to turn our wills and lives over to God, instead of to drink, food, sex, money, or other compulsions. When someone slips back into old patterns, we remember, "There but for the grace of God go I." We can then help the stumbling person because she knows we've been there. We know how he feels!

Accepting our need for mercy and assuming responsibility for our betrayals and failures gives us the gift of empathy and graciousness. As we experience healing when others accept our messy lives, so we are called to heal others laying battered and broken on the road of life. Viewed in that light, mercy is evangelism at its very best.

> *Lord, make me an instrument of thy peace.*
> > *Where there is hatred, let me sow love;*
> > *Where there is injury, pardon;*
> > *Where there is despair, hope;*
> > *Where there is darkness, light;*
> > *Where there is sadness, joy.*
> *Divine Master, grant that I may not so much seek*
> > *To be consoled, as to console;*
> > *To be understood, as to understand;*
> > *To be loved, as to love.*
> > *For it is in giving that we receive;*
> > *It is in pardoning that we are pardoned;*
> > *It is in dying that we are born to eternal life.*
> > *Amen.*
>
> *—St. Francis of Assisi*

6

Blessed Are the Pure in Heart

How blest are those whose hearts are pure;
they shall see God. (NEB)

In his book, *The Way of the Heart,* Henri Nouwen tells the story of a peasant who asked a Russian mystic to teach him how to pray without ceasing. The old mystic told the young man to repeat the phrase "Lord Jesus Christ have mercy on me." He was to repeat it as he worked, sat, rocked, ate. Eventually, the old man assured him, the prayer would move from his mind into his heart. There its message would keep echoing long after he stopped consciously repeating the words to himself. In this way he would come to pray without ceasing.

Prayer has always been a struggle for me. So I decided to try this technique for myself. For weeks I prayed, "Lord Jesus Christ have mercy on me." I said the words as I drove, did the dishes, hung out clothes, weeded the garden. After some weeks I awoke one night with the Jesus prayer running through my mind like a spontaneous litany.

One day as I was ironing, repeating the words almost without thinking, I realized I'd been praying "Lord Jesus Christ have mercy." I was dropping the last two words, *on me*. With a start, I sensed the old saint's promise coming true in more ways than I had anticipated. Not only had the words of the prayer moved from my conscious to my unconscious but they had begun to change me.

Deleting *on me* wasn't an oversight, I realized. I'd done it for a reason. Because I felt shaky about myself I didn't think I was worth praying for day after day. Even worse, I resisted those two little words because I didn't want to admit neediness and sin. Praying those two definitive words confronted my hidden arrogance and showed me my need for forgiveness and change.

By confronting me with my need for mercy, they showed me my impurities. By showing me my impurities, they set me on the road to purity of heart.

A Consistent Choice

Most of the translations of the Beatitudes vary widely. It's interesting that I found only one variation for the sixth beatitude, "Blessed are the pure in heart, for they will see God." The New Testament in Basic English uses the word *clean*. All others say *pure*.

Since so many translators chose "pure in heart" I headed straight for the dictionary to see what *pure* really implies. The French root means "bright, shining, clear." The Greek means "fire, purifying through heat." The Latin means "clear and concise."

The Little and Ives-Webster Dictionary (1963) defines *pure* like this:

> 1. free, not mixed with, clean, uncontaminated
> 2. morally clean; chaste in mind and thought; physically chaste
> 3. free from low, sordid, interested motives; candid, uncorrupted.
> 4. of a high uncorrupted standard, not decadent or debased.

Jesus really said a mouthful when he blessed the *pure*!

Purity Is a Process

Wait. Jesus doesn't start us on our spiritual journey by saying, "Blessed are the pure in heart." He starts by blessing those who know they're spiritually impoverished, or *impure*. Then he spells out subsequent steps.

Blessed are those who can mourn their experiences, those whom life has humbled, meeked, given a more realistic self-understanding.

Blessed are those who seek God's will for their lives. The Spirit will fill them with insight.

Blessed are the merciful, the considerate, the sensitive persons.

Taking the Beatitudes to heart, like working the Twelve Steps, often feels like stepping into the fiery furnace. So much in us needs to be burned away before we can experience purity of heart leading to happiness and serenity.

God's cleansing is gradual, however. It moves us

back and forth from attitude to action, always nudging us toward greater spiritual health.

Spiritual purity really begins when we decide to turn our will and our lives over to God's care and risk a searching and fearless moral inventory. Fortunately, we don't have to do anything right away. It's enough to take a good hard look at our many strengths and weaknesses.

But the time comes when we need to do something with that information. That's where Step Five comes in. We "admitted to God, to ourselves, and to another human being the exact nature of our wrongs." Accepting the need for change, and even admitting that need to another, doesn't right all wrongs or prompt us to take risks. But it helps.

God's way of bringing about change is often painful. We need to be ready to accept whatever comes. Even when we know our way isn't working, it's hard to give up our old ways of seeing ourselves and life. Step Six, we "were entirely ready to have God remove all these defects of character," helps us get used to the idea that we have to *want* to be pure in heart before we can ask God's help. Our readiness leads us to Step Seven, "humbly asked him to remove all of our shortcomings."

God doesn't have a magic wand. God never does for us what we need to do for ourselves. Thus God involves us in the change process. Before we can become pure of heart we have to accept responsibility for our choices and actions. We have to sort out *I can'ts* from *I won'ts*. One way to do that is to "make a list of all the people we had wronged"

(Step Eight). Then eventually we can "make amends whenever possible without hurting others"(Step Nine).

When the rich young ruler came to Jesus for help, Jesus knew that he had substituted wealth and comfort for spirituality. Jesus' advice jarred him. "Go and sell all you have and give the money to the poor, and come and . . . then follow me."

The Bible tells us the young man went away sorrowful. But who knows. Maybe he finally did follow Jesus' advice. Making amends is never easy. Sometimes we have to retrace our steps and grieve for our losses before we can go on.

Once we get accustomed to working the steps we don't have to make as many mistakes. We "continued to take personal inventory and when we were wrong promptly admitted it" (Step Ten), teaches us to deal with problems when they arise rather than letting molehills grow into mountains.

This practical approach to daily living prepares us for Step Eleven. We "sought through prayer and meditation to improve our conscious contact with God as we understood him, praying only for knowledge of his will for us and the power to carry that out."

Purity and Prayer

The time-honored methods for making contact with God are prayer and meditation. Both are crucial in our spiritual journey. Each serves a different purpose.

Many of us approach prayer as if our task is to

wake a distant or sleeping God. Yet we're the distant and indifferent ones. God wants us to pray because God is eager to communicate with us. God wants to arouse us from our spiritual lethargy. Prayer is God's idea, not ours. When we pray and meditate, confident that God is there for us, something truly wonderful happens.

Prayer is conversation with God. When we pray, we tell God what we're feeling, needing, worrying about, grateful for. We ask for guidance, direction, insight. We thank God for the challenges and rewards of life.

Once we've prayed, once we've talked with God and opened ourselves to divine guidance and input, then we can meditate. In meditation we stop talking. We listen. We turn off the mental clutter and static. As we learn to be quiet before God, we give God permission to enter our minds. Then we can hear God's reassurances and receive guidance.

People, Places, and Things

"Blessed are the pure in heart" doesn't command perfection. We never achieve perfection. Only God is perfect. Purity is a process to which we commit ourselves when we accept Christ as Savior and admit we need something or someone greater than ourselves.

Purity involves how we relate to and respond to our five senses. It involves what we deliberately allow ourselves to think, touch, watch, hear, and do.

Purity involves all these things: The kinds of music we listen to. The books we read. The programs we watch. The people with whom we associate. The food we eat. The church we attend. Where we work. How we spend our leisure time and money. Who we vote for.

We have far more control over our choices and attitudes than we want to admit. Purity has to do with choices. It has to do with persons, places, and things, and how much space we allow in our lives for God!

One of the cardinal rules for a recovering alcoholic or addict is to change people, places, and things. Our one child discovered the hard way why that has become such an important rule. After being in treatment two times, he still couldn't stay clean. This was because he was unwilling to leave behind the old people, places, and things. As a result he found himself picking up time after time. Not until he moved away from old haunts and friends, and associated with people in the program committed to their own sobriety, was he able to stay sober.

That principle holds true for us as growing Christians. We won't grow in faith and gentleness of spirit until we change the people, places, and things holding us back. This, incidentally, was the first piece of advice Paul received after his conversion.

Backing off from the people, places, and things that stand in our way shouldn't be done in judgmental or demeaning ways, however. It's enough quietly to recognize that this person, that activity, those interests are no longer good for me. They aren't helping me grow in gracefulness.

Blessed, happy, enviable are the pure in heart, for they shall see God. What we do, what we listen to, where we go, affects our spiritual development. We can pollute our minds and hearts with things we know are destructive. Or we can move away from those negative influences and reach out to God. We can then trust that God will fill the void. God will give us back the part of ourselves that was lost because of our inner pollution.

Our children won't stay drug and chemical free if they choose to spend their time in bars and partying. The person struggling to develop a healthy sexuality won't be able to respond in positive ways as long as he/she looks at pornography, frequents adult bookstores, or sleeps with multiple partners.

It's hard to desire purity, let alone become emotionally and spiritually uncontaminated as long as we think dirty and profane talk is smart. It's impossible to be pure of heart when we resent what happens to us and are ungrateful for the challenges life offers us. It's impossible when we choose to think the worst of others.

We won't find the gifts hidden in our varied experience if we always focus on the negative, choosing to interpret life, people, and events in pessimistic, judgmental, gossipy ways. We can't grow spiritually or experience the reality of God when we're too busy to meditate, pray, and read our Bible or other inspirational and devotional material.

Finding the Hidden Gift

One of the great benefits that came from our family addiction was learning to see the gift hiding behind the face of pain. Our society tells us things such as death, bankruptcy, divorce, addiction, and homosexuality are evil. The truth is that such things become evil when we allow them to destroy our hope and blot out our awareness of God.

The seemingly unacceptable are often the very things which bring us to God. The very thing that seemed so terrible to me—that my children were drug addicts and alcoholics—not only opened me to God in new ways but led my children to a relationship with their Higher Power. Sometimes we have to hit bottom before we can let go and let God begin to purify our lives.

It's difficult to praise God when things go wrong. But it's possible. While our purity cannot protect us from suffering, it can shape our responses and open us to see the hand of God in everything that happens. And isn't that exactly what Jesus promised would happen? The pure shall see God.

Learning to look for God helps us see God in everything. The point is not that God wills evil and suffering, but that God never abandons us. Behind everything God dwells, calling us to help transform and rise above even the most tragic events by choosing the path of love.

Because we experience God through our senses, our body is literally God's temple. We can step out in faith and stop smoking, drinking, and eating unhealthy foods. We can avoid gossip, choose to see good in the worst of situations, let go of our perfectionism and judgmentalism. We can practice thankfulness and praise. Then we'll discover that purity has to do with being willing to learn, to change, to grow, to think positively.

Purity involves using good judgment about what we do, where we go, with whom we spend our time, what we read and watch on TV. Most important, purity teaches us to praise God for everything that happens to us, good and bad. In striving to focus on finding the good in every situation. Then we'll see God in everything and everyone.

The apostle Paul restates the sixth beatitude in Phillipians 4:4-9.

> May you always be joyful in our union with the Lord. I say it again: rejoice. Show a gentle attitude toward everyone. The Lord is coming soon. Don't worry about anything, but in all your prayers ask God for what you need, always asking him with a thankful heart. And God's peace, which is far beyond human understanding, will keep your hearts and minds safe in union with Christ Jesus.
>
> In conclusion . . . fill your minds with those things that are good and that deserve praise: things that are true, noble, right, pure, lovely, and honorable. Put into practice what you learned and received from me, both from my words and from my actions. And the God who gives us peace will be with you.

The prayer of a 15th-century monk, Fra Giovanni, complements the beatitude.

There is nothing I can give you which you have not; but there is much, very much, that while I cannot give it, you can take.

No heaven can come to us unless our hearts find rest in today. Take heaven! No peace lies in the future which is not hidden in this present instant. Take peace!

The gloom of the world is but a shadow. Behind it, yet within is joy. There is radiance and glory in the darkness could we but see and to see we have only to look. I beseech you to look.

Life is so generous a giver, but we, judging its gifts by their covering, cast them away as ugly, or heavy, or hard. Remove the covering, and you will find beneath it a living splendor, woven of love, by wisdom, with power.

Welcome it, grasp it, and you touch the angel's hand that brings it to you. Everything we call a trial, a sorrow, a duty, is there, and the wonder of an overshadowing presence. Our joys, too, be not content with them as joys. They, too, conceal diviner gifts.

And so, at this time I greet you. Not quite as the world sends greetings, but with profound esteem, and with the prayer that for you now and forever, the day breaks, and the shadows flee away.

7

Blessed Are the Peacemakers

Blessed . . . are the makers and maintainers of peace, for they shall be called the sons [and daughters] of God. (AMP)

Insanity is the compulsion to persist with irrational or destructive behaviors even when they don't achieve the desired result. Thus war is insane. After thousands of years of fighting, after wars to end all wars, war, suffering, rebellion, and injustice persist. Violence can only beget more violence.

Yet world powers and even family systems continue to settle conflicts through violence. Our collective insanity keeps us from seeing clearly. As with all addictions (for war is an addiction), we rationalize our bizarre behavior. We not only insist our way is best, we assure each other that justice and non-violent solutions don't work. This denial is the devil's tool.

Luke's account of the Triumphal Entry has Jesus weep in the midst of the excitement and fanfare of his dramatic entry into the city.

He came closer to the city, and when he saw it, he wept over it, saying, "If you only knew today what is needed for peace! But now you cannot see it! The time will come when your enemies will surround you with barricades, blockade you, and close in on you from every side. They will completely destroy you and the people within your walls; not a single stone will they leave in its place, because you did not recognize the time when God came to save you!" (Luke 19:41-44)

"If you only knew what is needed for peace. . . !" But we *do* know. We just don't want to do it. We (myself included) haven't rejected nonviolence because it doesn't work. We've rejected nonviolent solutions because they ask too much of us. They demand we do something different.

Nonviolent methods require creativity and self-sacrifice. They require looking beyond symptoms to root causes of conflict. They put the onus back on us, not on the so-called enemy. This is because as peacemakers we can't insist that someone else make life safe for us so we don't have to take risks.

Peacemaking not only requires us to change but to make the first move. Fear, apathy, and despair are symptoms of our lack of trust in God's ability or willingness to meet our basic needs. Remember that list of the seven deadly sins and the fears involved?

> Pride is a fear of the truth.
> Greed is a fear of being in need.
> Lust is a fear of rejection.

Anger is a fear of being hurt, disappointment.
Gluttony is a fear of being in want.
Envy is a fear of accepting ourselves as we are.
Laziness is a fear of responsibility.

Our fears cause violence. They keep us from being open to changes. We think we have to solve everything by ourselves—but know we can't. We despair. In our despair and unwillingness to admit our powerlessness, we lash out. We feel the Jesus Way isn't realistic. But how do we know when we're afraid to try?

Peacemaking Can Create Conflict

Change in one person forces change in others. Those whom change threatens will try to discredit and destroy the agents of change. Just by doing what's right in a given situation, we become change agents calling others to change. This is why the Beatitudes and the Twelve Step approach of focusing on ourselves instead of the offender is so effective in the long run.

Unfortunately, this is also why the immediate result of detaching from conflict and doing something different often intensifies tension. Peacemaking may at first seem to escalate conflict rather than yield immediate reconciliation or change.

Change doesn't come easily. It requires time. Even our families and close friends may not understand or condone our actions when we claim the promises of God or begin going to Twelve Step Meetings. Witness the stress tax-resistance and non-registration has caused within the Mennonite church, which is proud of being a historic peace church.

Ironically, we can get so used to living with conflict, chaos, and pain that it becomes comfortable. Many in Al-Anon admit it was easier living with drunk family members than adjusting to their sobriety. It's easier to live with the existing situation than go through the agony of changing our whole approach to life and self.

"Never think I have come to bring peace upon the earth. No, I have not come to bring peace but a sword! For I have come to set a man against his own father, a daughter against her own mother. . ." (Matthew 10:34-35, NTME). To use these words of Christ to justify war and other forms of violence completely distorts his meaning. With this graphic description of what often happens when one in a family makes a commitment to Christ and others don't, Jesus points out that conflict is an integral part of life. Change is threatening because it places demands on everyone.

In this passage, as in others, Jesus also reminds us faithfulness doesn't always bring a happy ending. The good don't always live happily ever after. Nor does peacemaking imply the end of evil or that our enemies will welcome our shaky gestures to make amends.

Make no mistake. The Jesus way is threatening. In spite of our illusions, we can't co-exist unchanged with Christ. Either we die to ourselves and our old ways of doing things or we discredit and destroy Jesus. Witness the cross.

So why should we work for peace? What's the point? Why get involved?

Because God calls us to be peacemakers.

Because in the long run it works.

Because allowing Jesus to transcend and transform us gives us peace of mind and heart, regardless of what's going on around us.

Because the Jesus way gives us better tools for dealing with life's inevitable pain and stress.

Because when we're at peace with ourselves, we set in motion little ripples of serenity that affect others and draw them to us.

Peacemaking has to do with our attitudes and actions. It involves how we treat ourselves, our possessions, the environment, others, God. It means taking seriously the Step Twelve, which reads: "Having had a spiritual awakening as a result of these steps, we tried to carry this message to others and to practice these principles in all our affairs."

In the biblical perspective there can be no peace apart from forgiveness, justice, mercy, and a meeked, disciplined humility. In fact, an alternative translation for this beatitude could be "Blessed are they who give up everything they have to lovingly work for justice."

I once heard Hugo Zorilla, a Colombian pastor and theologian, tell a Canadian audience, "The real issues of peace don't focus on violence versus nonviolence, but on justice versus injustice. Limiting peace to the simple cessation of violence is our way of avoiding what is truly at stake."

What if the stakes are too high? Is justice even

possible in an unjust world? And what do we do with the Old Testament stories which glorify war and even picture God as commander in chief ordering the Israelites to do some pretty awful and unjust things?

Despite first impressions, those stories aren't told to justify war, stock-piling war machinery, or adopting violent solutions to the conflicts of life—even when international boundaries are at stake. They're told to illustrate what happens when a people obey or disobey their sovereign God.

They're told so we can see ourselves in David, Gideon, and others who felt so small and helpless that they leaned on God's power rather than their own. They're told to remind us that when we rely on God rather than ourselves, we needn't fear the enemies.

The Beatitudes and Twelve Steps prepare us for our ultimate purpose in life—making real God's resurrection power in the world. They prepare us to take God so seriously we become pure, meeked, reconciling sons and daughters of the Prince of Peace! As Jesus reminds us

> Never be afraid of those who can kill the body but are powerless to kill the soul! Far better to stand in awe of the one who has the power to destroy body and soul in the fires of destruction!" (Matthew 10:28, NTME).

Violence, Addiction, and Denial

The ways we use the Bible to support our own views and actions shows how easily we deny or rationalize away whatever threatens us. We detour around the scary and demanding aspects of Jesus' life, death, teachings, and resurrection. We create wondrous six-lane bypasses around them when they affect our wealth, security, safety, friendships, families, and power relationships.

We're like the addict who, denying the addiction, insists he has no problem. He persists in denial even after he's lost his job, is deeply in debt, beats up his wife and children, wakes up in his own vomit, has black-outs, and can't function without something to smoke, pop, shoot, or drink.

Our human capacity to deny reality, to avoid what we don't want to see, is awesome indeed! Think of all the times Jesus made the observation, "You have eyes that cannot see and ears that cannot hear. . . ." What a perfect description of denial, a tool we all use, addicts or not!

The changes needed for world and domestic peace are so simple yet so radical that we choose not to acknowledge them. We don't want to be the ones who have to change. After all, we reason, if the others would shape up, I wouldn't feel bad. If everyone else would do what they should, we wouldn't have all these problems. If they did something, I'd see change was worth the effort and do some changing myself.

It's easier to rely on war and violence, racism and sexism* than face just how sick our affluent life style has made us. Not only does our denial make us turn our sickness into a holy crusade and blame others for world problems, our fear and paranoia make us crucify anyone who dares to challenge our values and rationalizations or our economic, political, and military systems. It's so much easier to project blame outside of ourselves, to see the causes of evil and bloodshed as coming from someone or something other than ourselves.

In the late 1980s dramatic changes took place in Eastern Europe. Their outcome remains in doubt at the time of this writing. If freedom continues to sweep across the communist world, old mentalities and policies may yet die.

But until communism began to tremble, United States foreign policy was based on the premise that communism was responsible for the world's ills. And if communism hardens, its role as scapegoat will no doubt be important again. Or we may look for other scapegoats.

Whatever scapegoats we might like to blame, we might find truer culprits if we looked more closely at ourselves. The United States hosts one of the world's more greedy and violent societies. We hide from that reality through many rationalizations.

Because we have a democratic government, committed to noble values, we reason that it's all right for us to consume most of the world's resources and exploit poor people at home and abroad.

What the free market demands we feel justified in producing, even if the demand is for guns and bombs. Yet we're appalled when others, having learned shallow moral reasoning from us, use the very weapons we sold them against us!

There are other examples of insane thinking that

even Christians rarely question. As private citizens we want law and order, yet we demand the right to own and use guns. We vote down any legislation that outlaws or limits our immediate access to objects of terror.

We glorify individualism and violence, luxury and instant gratification.

We're horrified at the high rate of illegitimate births, yet we resist sex education and birth control.

We promote alcohol and medications as the desired solution to stress and distress without connecting them with our drug epidemic.

We reject day-care centers, education, food, health-care, clothing, jobs, homes for the homeless, mental health care and birth control facilities, and drug treatment programs as too expensive. Yet we put trillions into war machinery.

As a nation and a church we're addicted to affluence and violence! As with any addiction, we quickly become paranoid. We glorify our military leaders, gang lords, and violent lawmen. We downgrade our teachers, social workers, Peace Corp volunteers, prison reformers, advocates for the poor, Martin Luther King, Mother Teresa. Our favorite sports and entertainment reek with violence.

Let's be honest. Our way isn't working. Divorces outnumber marriages. The incidence of drug and alcohol addiction, wife and child abuse, and incest is soaring. Racial unrest, crime, and the rape of our land dominate the headlines. The numbers of homeless and unemployed right in our own communities grow and grow. Something has gone terribly awry.

Focusing on problems in other countries won't make ours go away. We can't fix others until we fix ourselves. Change starts with us.

A Different Option

The Twelve Steps offer church and society, as well as individuals, a way to become peacemakers. The program's systematic approach summarizes the basic philosophy of Jesus' teachings. It helps us see with new eyes and hear with new ears. By applying these steps to our business, national, and international relationships as well as our private lives, we could actually turn this war-torn, fear-riddled world upside down.

Jesus taught that working on ourselves, whether as individuals or nations, is both the best and finally the easiest way to change. Because try as we will, we can't change others. We can only change ourselves.

What would it mean to "Twelve-step" our way to peace? What would happen if the United States, for instance, took care of its own homeless, needy, and disenfranchised before it demanded that others do the same?

As a way of illustrating how comprehensive the Twelve Step principles are, let's reword them to apply to national issues. We can remember, as we do so, that we simultaneously have to take these steps in our own personal lives and relationships and local communities.

(1) We admitted we were powerless over our love of power and our addiction to violence. We confessed our social structures, bureaucracy, and the budget deficit had become unmanageable.

(2) We came to believe that a Power greater than ourselves could restore us to sanity as a people and a nation.

(3) We decided to turn our will and lives over to the care of God instead of to the state, industry, Pentagon, or other powers that be.

(4) Instead of focusing on what the communists or others are doing wrong and using their abuses as an excuse for what we do, we made a searching and fearless moral inventory of ourselves. We faced our own injustices, poor policies, and violations of human rights.

(5) We admitted to God, ourselves, and others the exact nature of our national and political wrongs.

(6) We were entirely ready to have God remove all our private, social, religious, and national character defects.

(7) We humbly asked God to remove our shortcomings.

(8) We made a list of all persons, races, groups, and countries we had harmed. We became willing to make amends to them all.

(9) We made direct amends to such people, nations, and groups whenever possible, except when to do so would injure them or others.

(10) We continued to take personal and national inventory. When we were wrong in pursuing a par-

ticular policy, we promptly admitted it.

(11) We sought through prayer and meditation to improve our conscious contact with God as we understood God. We prayed only for knowledge of God's will for us and the power to carry that out.

(12) Having had a spiritual awakening as a result of these steps, we tried to carry this message of world peace, brotherhood, equality, and justice to all persons and countries. We aimed to practice these principles in all our affairs.

We can't change others. We can change ourselves! There is so much power in that simple statement. When we change ourselves we stir change in those around us. When we no longer play by the old rules, react in familiar ways, or buy into commonly accepted values, this throws others off balance.

Marriages can be saved, for instance, even if one partner refuses to go for counseling. When one partner works at becoming more responsible, less critical, and more self-assertive, things shift.

One partner can stop focusing on the other's reactions or no longer covers up for the other's inadequacies. She can assume responsibility for her own feelings. He can stop blaming his spouse for his unhappiness. Then the relationship will change. The noncooperating partner can't function as he or she once did when the other stops playing the old games.

The same is true for any conflict situation, whether in a church, organization, political party, or nation. Suppose each company did what it could

to be environmentally responsible rather than trying to get away with as little as possible or waiting
for someone else to go first? This would greatly re-
duce waste disposal and air pollution problems.

A Life-changing Choice

The Ghandis of the world are much more threatening and powerful than any military commander.
Their quiet insistence on what is just and right, and
their willingness to die themselves rather than to
cause others to die, holds up a mirror to the rest of
the world. The world sees its ugliness reflected
back.

It is this characteristic (holding up the mirror
that allows us to see ourselves) that makes Jesus
and the peace teachings so threatening even in the
church. By going to the cross, Jesus turned his back
on violence and our conventional perceptions of
power. He called our denials and rationalizations
into question. By daring to live and die for what he
believed, he forced us to face our own hypocrisy.

There is something credible though unnerving
about this saying:

> You have heard that it was said "An eye for an eye,
> and a tooth for a tooth." But now I tell you: Do not
> take revenge on someone who wrongs you. If any-
> one slaps you on the right cheek, let him slap your
> left cheek too. And if someone takes you to court
> to sue you for your shirt, let him have your coat as
> well. And if one of the occupation troops forces
> you to carry his pack one mile, carry it two miles"
> (Matthew 5:38-41).

We alone are responsible for the ways we respond to situations, persons, and problems. Others can hurt us but can't control our responses. They can't make us hate them, be bitter, or vengeful. We do that ourselves. Thus Jesus reminds us to get our own house in order before we try to change others.

> Whoever is angry with his brother will be brought to trial. Whoever calls his brother a worthless fool will be in danger of going to the fire of hell. So . . . make peace with your brother (Matt. 5:21-23).

> Forgive us the wrongs we have done, as we forgive the wrongs others have done to us (Matthew 6:12).

> Do not judge others, so that God will not judge you (Matthew 7:1).

> Put your sword back in its place. . . . All who take the sword will die by the sword (Matthew 26:52).

> Love your enemies . . . do good to those who do evil (Matthew 5:43-48).

> You cannot serve both God and money (Matthew 6:24).

> Do not be worried about the food and drink you need. . . . After all, isn't life worth more than food? (Matthew 6:25).

Being broken and fallible, and despite our best intentions, we'll at times slip back into our old patterns and ways of thinking. We'll forget we're powerless over our compulsions. We'll forget and try to run others' lives. We'll forget God is in control, inviting us to place our wills and lives in divine hands. We'll forget only God can restore us to sanity. We'll forget to be merciful and pure in heart, to hunger and thirst after righteousness instead of success or money or popularity or a new car. We'll forget to take our own inventory and allow God to meek us; we'll instead expect others to be meeked so we won't have to work so hard ourselves.

Yes, we will slip. That's why it's important to go to meetings and church, to pray and meditate, to read devotional and Twelve Step material. That's why we need each other in the church or program to be strong for us when we are weak.

Peace, Praise, and Sacrifice

In Hebrews 13:15 we read, "Let us, then, always offer praise to God." Most of us in the United States and Canada aren't used to doing without. When we sacrifice something, we intentionally give up something prized or desirable for something that has a higher claim or value. That's why a thankful and praising heart is the most important sacrifice we can make. As we reach for the gift wrapped in our pain and conflict situations, as we praise God for our troubles, we give up the right to make things conform to our expectations and wishes.

When we let go and let God be in control, when we "always offer praise to God," we give up our rights to the very blessings and opportunities we think due us. We do this so that everyone, the world over, can live in peace and without want.

"Blessed are the peacemakers" calls us to sacrifice our right to the blessings we think due us. I had to give up my dream of a drug free family to get back a deeper understanding of God's redemptive activity in our lives. I had to give up my image of myself as the all-giving mother to see my children become the independent, caring responsible individuals I'd always wanted them to be.

The same principle applies on a national and world level. We may have to lower our standard of living, shrink the power of our multinational corporations, and stop selling arms to other countries. Then the world's poor will have a chance and we will live with less fear. Jesus reminded us that "a house divided against itself cannot stand." As long as we base our economy on instruments of terror, we'll be afraid, and with due cause!

We can't change the world or even those close to us, but we can change ourselves and become the persons God calls us to be. We can't end another's greed but can work on our own selfish and greedy impulses. We can't make others peaceful but we can curb our own violent impulses and seek new responses patterned after those we see in Christ.

As we open ourselves to change, as God works in our lives, we have an impact on others. God's life-changing influence flows from us like ripples in a pond. We become centered, serene, not easily threatened. We become peacemakers. Ripples of peace-power spread across the world!

Peace: Fact, Not Fantasy

Tragically few Christians, including those in my Anabaptist tradition, see peacemaking as integral to the Christian life and message. Yet this beatitude, "Happy are those who work for peace; God will call them his children!" calls us to claim our inheritance in God's family. God loves all God's children. Getting along with our siblings pleases our Parent. It makes life better for all.

In God's kingdom, peace and reconciliation are the realities. War is the illusion. Peace is of God. War is of the devil. When God is in charge, all things are made new, including our very selves.

Look at what Gandhi accomplished when he took Jesus seriously, or Martin Luther King, or William Penn—not to mention the long line of Christian martyrs and saints down through the ages. Growing up in Pennsylvania, I learned in my history classes that no Indian wars afflicted the state as long as the Quakers were in power. It was only after others came with guns and different views that the Indian wars broke out in the Pennsylvania territories.

Peace can't work? In Paraguay, civil war was averted and the Indians not exterminated because the Mennonite settlers refused to take sides. They ministered instead to everyone in need. What about the influence Mennonite Disaster Service, Mennonite Central Committee, and countless other service organizations have had? Think of Mother Teresa, David Livingston, Albert Schweitzer, and all the others who have gone out to love rather than hate, to heal rather than destroy. Peace a fantasy? Oh we of little faith!

In the early 1970s, Dr. H. A. Fast made an impassioned plea to the Commission on Home Ministries of the General Conference Mennonite Church to keep the Department for Peace and Justice active despite criticism. Through tears he cried out

> In my lifetime I've lived through five wars. Five major wars! The Spanish-American War, the First World War, the Second World War, the Korean Conflict, and now the Vietnam War! Enough is enough! It's time *we* say "no" to war in whatever form it takes, be it tax resistance, registration resistance, refusing to serve in the armed services, or not working for companies that have war contracts. . .!

> If every Mennonite dared to speak out against war, if every Mennonite cared enough to say no, regardless of the consequences; if every Mennonite was willing to be jailed, there wouldn't be prisons enough to hold us all. But even if there were, the world would never be the same after hearing the sounds of "Praise God from Whom All Blessings Flow" ringing from the prison cells.

If every Mennonite, if every Christian. . . . But the implications of "Happy are those who work for peace" is that I don't have to wait for every Mennonite or every Christian before I can do anything. I am enough. *I* can promote change.

If I trust God enough to turn my will and life over to divine care and guidance, the words of the seventh beatitude become true in me. If I acknowledge that Jesus stands at the door of my heart and knocks, asking to come in, I can show that indeed all peacemakers truly are blessed.

> *Oh God, help me take seriously the promise of the angels when they came to those poor, outcast shepherds on the hillside that first Christmas Day. "Don't be afraid! I am here with good news for you, which will bring great joy to all the people."*
>
> *God, give me serenity to accept the things I cannot change, courage to change the things I can, and wisdom to know the difference.*
>
> *Oh God, let there be peace on earth and let it begin with me. Amen.*

Blessed Are the Persecuted

*Happy are those who are persecuted because
they do what God requires;
the Kingdom of heaven belongs to them!*

And so our spiritual journey leads us forward, giving us the strength and serenity to accept the results of our choices and actions. But even as the Beatitudes help us develop the spiritual muscle to influence others for peace, justice, and reconciliation, they often set us at odds with other people. In this last beatitude Jesus reminds us it won't always be easy doing what we sense is right. Others may not approve; they may actively oppose us.

The growing tendency in our Western culture to blame and sue others makes it hard for us to respond to life's challenges. For instance, we want the benefits of technology and medical science but without the side effects. When anything goes wrong, we shift the blame from our own participation in what has happened. But blaming doesn't work.

Jesus ends his list of "to be attitudes" with "Be happy and glad, for a great reward is kept for you in heaven." He assures us that while we may not live to see our dreams come true in this life, our energy and efforts to work for good will pay off in the long run. God will have the last word. The whole picture is a lot bigger than we can see. Therefore we can't predict how our actions will affect the future.

One can't read *The Martyrs Mirror* and its stories of Anabaptist martyrs, Dietrich Bonhoeffer's *Letters from Prison*, Victor Frankl's *Man's Search for Meaning*, *The Diary of Anne Frank*, or Corrie ten Boom's *The Hiding Place* without sensing the joy and serenity these people felt as they faced persecution and death. Every action has its reaction. Every choice its specific outcome.

Accepting the Consequences

Many of us try to avoid responsibility and its consequences by not making decisions. Yet not to decide is to decide for the status quo. That old excuse "I can't" is really another way of saying "I won't."

Everything we do has consequences. Some are positive and some are negative, but there they always are. Jesus knew from experience that even when they persecute and kill us, our enemies can't rob us of what gives life meaning. They can't take from us knowing that we've done our best, that we've been true to ourselves and our beliefs.

Paul shared this insight:

> We are honored and disgraced; we are insulted and
> praised. . . . Although punished, we are not killed;
> although saddened, we are always glad; we seem
> poor, but we make many people rich; we seem to
> have nothing, yet we really possess everything"
> (2 Corinthians 6:8-10).

"Blessed are those who are persecuted" isn't a call
to martyr our way into heaven. It reminds us to accept graciously the inevitable results of our beliefs,
attitudes, and choices, especially those involving
"hungering and thirsting after righteousness." Jesus
came to give life: bubbling, contagious, serendipi-
tous life! He didn't come to make us miserable.

Yet anytime we choose to be different, some will
feel threatened and react negatively. Sometimes
that's to our advantage, sometimes not. Learning to
accept what happens without blaming or whining is
vital to our happiness and serenity.

Not only do we have to accept the consequences
of our own actions. We need to allow others to accept the consequences of theirs. Bearing another's
burdens sometimes means letting people find their
own answers instead of solving problems for them.
In the Twelve Step Program we avoid giving others
advice. We instead share what has worked for us as
a way of giving others new options.

Servanthood and discipling are central to Christian ethics. Yet Christ's call to be there for others
needn't mean doing something. Often it's enough to
connect people with needed resources. At other

times we need to get out of the way so they can learn the lessons life has to teach. Sometimes we serve best as we simply model change and resourcefulness in our own lives. But Christian discipling always involves believing in others and listening without judging.

Allowing others to experience the results of their choices and actions is basic to any Twelve Step Program. An addict's or alcoholic's recovery can't begin until they stop blaming others for their addiction and accept how they're hurting themselves and others. As long as family members and friends intervene, they not only allow the individual to remain addicted. They also further erode the addict's already devastated self-esteem. They send the message "We don't trust you to control your own life and destiny."

Co-dependency and Enabling

Family members of addicted or compulsive persons are called *co-dependents*. There is a reason for this. When one person in the family is sick, everyone else gets pulled into that sickness in one form or another.

Situations involving addictions can suck even the most enlightened persons into negative patterns. Trying to restore sanity to an insane situation, co-dependents take over the jobs and functions of the addicted person. In a short time, co-dependents become dependent on the abuser's maladjustment. This is because they focus all their time and energy on the abuser. The abuser becomes a key source of their identity.

Let me illustrate. Because I cared about my children I thought my unhappiness proved I loved them. I was caught up in the irrational thinking that is so much a part of addictions. So I couldn't see that every time I allowed my children to manipulate, abuse, or hurt me, I added one more bad memory to the already long list with which they would have to live! I didn't see that every time I did something for them they should have done themselves, I kept them from learning important skills.

By going to meetings I learned my life needn't revolve around my children's disease. I discovered my needs were as important as theirs. I realized I hadn't caused and therefore couldn't cure their drug use. I also came to see something profound (which relates to this last beatitude): I could allow myself happiness and fulfillment even if my children remained addicted.

Anytime we do for people something they should do for themselves, we keep them from learning the lessons life has to teach them. In the Program, taking over for another by trying to protect or control the situation is called *enabling*.

Many of us *enable* because we want to be helpful. We think the best way to help is to fix what hurts. However, sometimes we enable to cope with our own anxiety. Not being able to control others makes us anxious. By trying to change them and to fix their problems, we feel more secure, in control. As long as we do that, we don't have to face our fears and change.

Instead of helping our dysfunctional family members by letting them lie in the bed they make, however rumpled, we keep them from learning coping skills. We short-circuit the healing that comes with remorse and grief. We deflect the consequences that could have befallen them. Instead of helping them become stronger, we undermine their self-confidence, making it easier for them to continue their addiction.

A basic lesson I had to learn as a parent of drug abusers was that protecting my children from school authorities, the police, or bill collectors didn't help them. Trusting them to take responsibility for their own lives meant I stopped excusing their absences from school and paying their fines, car loans, and insurance premiums.

Sometimes they ended up driving an uninsured vehicle without a valid driver's license! Sometimes they missed work or had to walk. That was hard for me to handle. Not only did I have a healthy fear of the law, my image of the good parent was one who made the world safe for her children and did lots of caretaking things for them.

Taking Care of Ourselves

Somewhere along the line we have confused peace and goodness with the absence of conflict and dissension. But the issue isn't whether or not conflict erupts. The issue is how we deal with it when it does flare. "Blessed are the persecuted" reminds us that standing up for our beliefs will lead to conflict and disagreement at times.

Demanding that others live up to their God-given potential is equally controversial. Yet difficult as it is to stand up for what we believe, it's often harder not to. Conflict avoidance doesn't really help anyone in the end. In fact, we often suffer more when we run from conflict than when we grit our teeth and take a stand.

Turning our son's drug paraphernalia over to the authorities was one of the more difficult things I've ever done. Not only did being responsible for his arrest clash with my concept of parenting, it exposed our dirty linen to the public.

Yet once our son was arrested and the wheels of justice began grinding, it soon became clear we were all going to benefit. He received the help he needed in a court-mandated treatment facility. We got much needed family counseling and relief from tension. And it was actually easier to meet people because we were no longer living a lie.

I've discovered that the worst that can happen isn't that bad after all. Before our son's arrest, much of my energy went into denying the problem and covering up what was happening. Then the very thing I feared turned out to be a gift. Sure we had to swallow our pride. But once we did our friends and family supported and encouraged us. Given the mess the world is in, an important thing we can do as Christians is model the reality of honest confession, forgiveness, and resurrection in our own lives.

Despite my earlier fear of what others would think, my son's arrest increased my effectiveness as a pastor. Others not only saw us suffer. They watched us confront what was going on without allowing it to destroy us. Certainly some were critical and questioned my right to remain in leadership. They thought ministers should be immune to life's struggles. But most were supportive.

Most important for my ministry, the humbling we experienced opened me to others in new ways. Having experienced the freedom that forgiveness and a new start offers, I became less critical and more sensitive. As a bonus, my exposure to the Twelve Step Program enhanced my counseling and listening skills. Each experience, each lesson brings its own unexpected consequence.

I have to smile when people tell me I'm courageous for speaking in public about our experiences. I'm not being courageous. I'm taking care of myself. I suffered far more when I was trying to pretend nothing was wrong. By taking the offensive and telling my story openly, I ask people to meet me on my own terms. I can stress important concepts like alcoholism as an illness. Writing and speaking reminds me recovery is a process. It's also a way I can make amends to those we have hurt.

Betraying Ourselves

Having others betray or malign us is difficult. Far worse is the betrayal we inflict on ourselves when we violate our own principles and run from doing what we know is right. The price of righteous living may be high. The price of running from righteousness is even higher!

Suffering, especially emotional suffering, rarely

comes from what others say or do. We suffer from what we do to ourselves. We suffer from the ways we interpret events, the messages we send ourselves, the ways we try to please others or buy into their views or interpretations.

Coming Full Circle

Both Step Nine and Step Twelve relate directly to the last beatitude. Step Nine calls us to make amends for wrongs done. Step Twelve encourages us to share the good news and use the insights and tools we've gained in our relationships with others.

Pain is part of life. Things happen. Accidents occur. People react. When we do what we understand to be right, others may hurt us. But the last beatitude does more than warn us that the world doesn't like the way goodness exposes its evil to the light. It goes beyond reminding us that we must choose our response to pain.

It shows how the steps to hope create a *spiral*. When we respond to pain by admitting our need for God, we threaten others. This causes us more pain. Then we have to admit an even deeper need for God. As we cycle through continually deepening pain and reliance on God, our lives spiral ever upward toward Christian maturity.

Detachment: Gateway to Serenity

Detachment is an important concept in AA and FA circles. Learning to detach is a very helpful skill for everyone, whether living with an alcoholic or not. Detaching with love can give us the distance and emotional space we need to evaluate what is going on. Then we can make constructive changes instead of just reacting to our pain.

For instance, when others criticize us, we often hear them as rejecting us or judging our competence and worth. Anger or depression then takes over as a defense mechanism.

When someone is nasty, we can remind ourselves she or he is sharing valuable information about how they think, however unkind their method of delivery. Criticism tells us how others feel about a wide variety of subjects, including us. When we let criticism hurt instead of teaching us, we deny ourselves valuable chances to grow.

Detaching is an alternative to suffering. When we detach, we detach from the *behavior*, not the person. Detaching eliminates our need to withdraw, attack, or take sides. Hearing criticism while detached gives us important choices and the empowerment choice offers.

When I'm detached I ask, Whose problem is it, yours or mine? What is a correct response? Does this situation require me to change? Or is listening and valuing your views enough? How can I profit from this information, from your reaction? How can I use this experience to help others and myself?

Taking Ourselves Seriously

Most Christians are good accommodators. We want to be liked. We equate our self-worth and faith with pleasing people and avoiding conflict. Having someone angry at us makes us uneasy. We even equate Christianity with passivity and unassertiveness. Yet Jesus tells us we can't please both God and people. We have to make choices, even if that means standing alone or risking rejection.

An important aspect of the faith journey is learning to think for ourselves, to make decisions based on what we believe rather than what others tell us. It involves learning to trust our own instincts and intuitions about what to do.

Living in relationship means living with ourselves as well as others. We'll spend every moment of our lives with ourselves. We go to bed with ourselves every night and get up with ourselves every morning. To realize that is to see the importance of taking ourselves and our needs and values seriously.

Jesus reminds us we can be blessed, truly glad, when we're true enough to ourselves to live at peace with our choices and actions. Such spiritual and emotional integrity is what sets apart prophets and saints.

God's Consequences

Each beatitude ends with a consequence or outcome. Jesus promises that when we turn to God, God will meet our basic needs.

Let's do a quick review of our journey through the beatitudes by looking at how we profit from implementing each in our lives.

1. *Happy are those who know they are spiritually poor; the Kingdom of heaven belongs to them!*

The word "kingdom" is somewhat confusing because we tend to think of the "kingdom" as a place or a thing. It is, rather, a source of power. What Jesus is saying when he speaks of the "kingdom of heaven" is that as we turn to God, God will empower our living.

2. *Happy are those who mourn; God will comfort them!*

When we can be honest and open about our true feelings, when we can value and listen to our pain and grief, we'll receive the comfort and help we need to move beyond it.

3. *Happy are those who are humble; they will receive what God has promised!*

When we allow God to humble us, to meek and shape us, God gives us the tools and resources we need to become responsible productive individuals.

4. *Happy are those whose greatest desire is to do what God requires; God will satisfy them fully!*

When we seek to do what is right, to focus on our relationships with God, self, and others, life opens to us in new ways. We feel fulfilled and connected to life because we're literally filled with the Holy Spirit, who leads and guides us in the paths of righteousness.

5. *Happy are those who are merciful to others; God will be merciful to them!*

When we reach out with love and empathy, when we don't judge others, those same qualities come back to us.

6. *Happy are the pure in heart; they will see God!*

When we look for the good, for the promise and opportunity that lies in everything that happens, when we thank and affirm God in the midst of our pain, we are purified. Then we come to hear and see God in everything and everyone.

7. *Happy are those who work for peace; God will call them his children!*

As we gain new Christ-centered meaning and purpose and skills for our lives, we experience the freedom that comes in making friends instead of enemies. We lose both our fear of living and dying. We become confident of our connection with God.

8. *Happy are those who are persecuted because they do what God requires; the Kingdom of heaven belongs to them!*

When we accept the consequences of our choices and actions, we finally live joyously. Very much part of the world, yet not unduly influenced by it, we respond in appropriate and creative ways. In our times of testing, God stands with us. God blesses us with the "fruits of the Spirit" such as patience, love, joy, humility, mercy, and forgiveness.

> *Lord, how grateful I am that you permit us to experience the consequences of our choices and actions. Help me face my life's challenges without whining or shame, no matter what I have done, for with you all things are possible. Even my sins you redeem, my failures becoming the very stepping-stones to new life.*
>
> *Lord, empower me to let go and let you be in control. Teach me to number my days in joy and gratitude. Amen.*

Appendix

Selected Twelve Step Readings

Central to any Twelve Step Program are approved readings and devotional materials. These materials are designed to reinforce the concepts shared at meetings. They help flesh out the terse statements of the Twelve Steps. Some of these readings are used at every meeting. Others are found in various Twelve Step publications or have become important parts of particular Twelve Step treatment plans.

I've found the readings to be extremely helpful in my spiritual pilgrimage of faith. Along with my Bible, I read some Twelve Step materials everyday, borrowing most heavily from those connected with AA, Al-Anon, and FA. The ones I've included here have been extremely significant to me in my journey from despair to hope and hope to serenity.

I've chosen them, however, not only to give a feel of what Twelve Step material is like, but because these particular pieces reflect and restate the basic insights of the Sermon on the Mount and the Beatitudes.

Symptoms of Drug or Alcohol Abuse

If you believe someone in your family may be using drugs or alcohol, here is a list of symptoms drug or alcohol abuse cause in some but not all people.

1. Change in attitude or behavior patterns.
2. Red streaked eyes.
3. Dilated pupils.
4. Use of sprays or gum to cover smoke odors or to cover breath.
5. Obnoxious or belligerent attitudes which are often blamed on adolescence.
6. Withdrawal from family life or functions.
7. Lack of motivation; loss of interest in doing things.
8. Sleeps long hours during the day or "crashes." Disturbed sleep patterns.
9. May chill easily, have the shakes.
10. Goes right to own room upon entering house and closes door.
11. Sneaks out at night after curfew.
12. Loss of appetite or obsessed with sweets and junk foods.
13. Blames others for her or his problems at home, school, or work.
14. Pills missing at home.
15. Unexplained dents in car blamed on hit and run, etc.

16. Poor skin color; pale, pasty, rashes.
17. Slurred speech or rapid speech with no pauses. Flat expressionless speech.
18. Poor memory or impaired ability to concentrate.
19. Can lie to you and swear they are telling the truth.
20. Decreasing performance at school, work, or sports.
21. Frequent absences.
22. Uses incense in rooms.
23. Wearing sunglasses at inappropriate times.
24. Associating with known drug users.
25. Stomach or colon problems.
26. Nausea, sweating, trembling; signs of mononucleosis.
27. Acute anxiety accompanied by paranoid thoughts.
28. Sore throats, bronchial cough, runny nose, asthmatic wheezing, chest pains.

Helping

My role as helper is not to do things for the person I am trying to help, but to be things; not to try to control and change his actions, but through understanding and awareness, to change my reactions. I will change my negatives to positives; fear to faith; contempt for what he does to respect for the potential within him; hostility to understanding; and manipulation or overprotectiveness to release with love, not trying to make him fit a standard or image, but giving him an opportunity to pursue his own destiny, regardless of what his choice maybe.

I will change my dominance to encouragement; panic to serenity; the inertia of despair to the energy of my own personal growth; and self-justification to self-understanding.

Self-pity blocks effective action. The more I indulge in it, the more I feel that the answer to my problem is a change in others and in society, not in myself. Thus I become a hopeless case.

Exhaustion is the result when I use my energy in mulling over the past with regret, or in trying to figure ways to escape a future that has yet to arrive. Projecting an image of the future and anxiously hovering over it, for fear that it will or it won't come true uses all of my energy and leaves me unable to live today. Yet living today is the only way to have a life.

I will have no thought for the future actions of others, neither expecting them to be better or worse as time goes on, for in such expectations I am really trying to create. I will love and let be.

All people are always changing. If I try to judge them, I do so only on what I think I know of them, failing to realize that there is much I do not know. I will give others credit for attempts at progress and for having had many victories which are unknown.

I, too, am always changing, and I can make that change a constructive one, if I am willing. I can change myself. Others I can only love.

—Families Anonymous, Inc.
P.O. Box 528
Van Nuys, CA 91408
818-989-7841

One Day at a Time

There are two days in every week about which we should not worry; two days which should be kept free from fear and apprehension.

One of these days is Yesterday, with its mistakes and cares, its faults and blunders, its aches and pains. Yesterday passed forever beyond our control. All the money in the world cannot bring back Yesterday. We cannot undo a single act we performed; we cannot erase a single word. Yesterday is gone!

The other day we should not worry about is Tomorrow with its possible burdens, its large promise and poor performance. Tomorrow is also beyond our immediate control; Tomorrow's sun will rise, either in splendor or behind a mask of clouds . . . but it will rise. Until it does, we have no stake in Tomorrow, for it is yet unborn.

This leaves only one day . . . Today! Any man can fight the battle of just one day. It is only when you and I have the burdens of those two awful eternities, Yesterday and Tomorrow . . . that we break down.

It is not the experiences of Today that drives men mad . . . it is the remorse or bitterness for something which happened Yesterday and the dread of what Tomorrow may bring.

Let us, therefore, live but one day at a time.

—Families Anonymous, Inc.

Just for Today

Just for today I will try to live this day only, and not tackle my whole life problem at once. I can do something for twelve hours that would appall me if I felt that I had to keep it up for a lifetime.

Just for today I will be happy. This assumes to be true what Abraham Lincoln said, "That most folks are as happy as they make up their minds to be."

Just for today I will adjust myself to what is, and not try to adjust everything to my own desires. . . .

Just for today I will try to strengthen my mind. I will study. I will learn something useful. I will not be a mental loafer. I will read something that requires effort, thought, and concentration.

Just for today I will exercise my soul in three ways; I will do somebody a good turn, and not get found out. . . . I will do at least two things I don't want to do—just for exercise. I will not show anyone that my feelings are hurt; they may be hurt, but today I will not show it.

Just for today I will be agreeable. I will look as well as I can, dress becomingly, talk low, act courteously, criticize not one bit, not find fault with anything, and not try to improve or regulate anybody except myself.

Just for today I will have a program. I may not follow it exactly, but I will have it. I will save myself from two pests; hurry and indecision.

Just for today I will have a quiet half hour all by myself, and relax. During this half hour, sometime, I will try to get a better perspective of my life.

Just for today I will be unafraid. Especially I will not be afraid to enjoy what is beautiful, and to believe that as I give to the world, so the world will give to me.   —Families Anonymous, Inc.

Bibliography

Brandt, Priscilla, *Two Way Prayer*, Waco, Tex.: Word Books, 1979

"Helping," Van Nuys, Calif.: Families Anonymous, Inc.

Jordan, Clarence, *Sermon on the Mount*, Valley Forge, Pa.: Judson Press, A Koinonia Publication, 1970

"Just for Today," Van Nuys, Calif.: Families Anonymous, Inc.

Milham, Richard, *Like It Is Today: Paraphrased Parables*, Nashville: Broadman Press, 1970

Miller, John W., *The Christian Way: A Guide to the Christian Life Based on the Sermon on the Mount*, Scottdale, Pa.: Herald Press, 1969

Nouwen, Henri J. M., *The Way of the Heart*, New York: The Seabury Press, 1981

"One Day at a Time," Van Nuys, Calif.: Families Anonymous, Inc.

The Twelve Steps of Alcoholics Anonymous (interpreted by The Hazelden Foundation). New York: Harper and Row, Publishers, Inc., 1987

Twelve Steps for Adult Children, San Diego: Recovery Publications, 1987

Richard Wilson, *The Journey of the Beatitudes*, United States, Hazelden, 1986

The Author

Joyce M. Shutt graduated from Bluffton College (Ohio) in 1958 with a degree in dramatic literature. She taught high school English for a year, then married her husband, Earl. Together they served two years with Mennonite Central Committee in Austria and Germany.

While in Austria, they met an American couple who had adopted mixed-race children left behind by American servicemen. This made a lasting impression on Joyce and Earl. Returning to the United States during the height of the civil rights movement, they adopted two biracial boys following the birth of two daughters.

For 27 years they have lived on a fruit farm in rural Adams County, Pennsylvania, close to Gettysburg. There they grow apples, cherries, and peaches.

From 1970 to 1982 Joyce served on the Literature

Committee for Women in Mission (General Conference Mennonite Church). She was one of the first women appointed to serve on the denomination's Commission on Home Ministries.

Joyce graduated from Gettysburg Lutheran Seminary in 1980 and began pastoring her home church that same year. Since her ordination in 1980, she has pastored the Fairfield Mennonite Church.

In 1986 she began work as part-time chaplain at Green Acres, an Adams County nursing home.